GROUP LIFE COACHING
BLUEPRINT

A Complete Guide to Creating a Group Life Coaching Business

Joeel A. Rivera, M.Ed.
& Natalie Rivera

ISBN 978-1-60166-051-0

*Find out how to become a Certified Group Life Coach
at the end of this book!*

TRANSFORMATION
PUBLISHING ——

CONTENTS

CHAPTER 1: YOUR GROUP COACHING BUSINESS

WHY GROUP COACHING?

Do you feel like you've naturally been coaching people your whole life? When you found out life coaching was an actual profession, were you like, "I didn't know I could get PAID for this! I'm in!" Do you want to be your own boss and be in control of your own schedule? Do you have a message to share and want to make a difference in the world? Do you feel drawn to help:

- Professionals who hate their job
- Managers who are overwhelmed
- Business owners who are struggling
- People who want to live healthy
- People who want to be better parents
- People who want to improve their relationships
- People who want to reach their potential

Being a life coach is a rewarding and fulfilling side hustle/business/career! If you're reading this, you are part of our tribe of heart-centered indiepreneurs and transformation junkies. Welcome home!

Are you new to life coaching? Or have you already started coaching and you're looking to add new tools to your coaching toolbox? Or, perhaps you have a thriving coaching business and you're looking for new strategies?

WHY DO YOU WANT TO DO GROUP COACHING?

- Reach more people

- Make more money
- Leverage your time better
- Tired/burnt out trying to fill your schedule with one-on-ones
- Grow your business faster
- Provide more value to your clients
- Offer a more affordable option for your clients
- Use as low-cost entry-level program in order to upsell to your coaching or signature program
- Use as a follow-up option for current or former clients

WHY WE RECOMMEND GROUP COACHING:

Unfortunately, most coaches end up leaving the field. Why? Because they're not making enough money and/or they burn out constantly stressing over how to get enough paying clients.

We were there ourselves, trying to juggle parenting, our time together as a couple, marketing and administrative time, and sessions with our coaching clients, all without feeling like we had to work 12-hour days or be on call all the time. Beginning group coaching was the #1 best decision we ever made in our business. Not only did it normalize our schedule, it also grew our income exponentially!

- Your income becomes much more predictable! You can look at your individual coaching clients as icing on the cake.
- Your income is no longer limited by how many hours a week you can schedule coaching one-on-one, and still manage to keep up with all of your other business and personal responsibilities, including tracking and serving your clients and marketing to get new ones.
- No more scheduling headaches! Trying to make your schedule fit with your clients' schedule can be a real challenge. You may want to take off evenings, but then you get clients who work full-time jobs and can *only* meet in the evenings (just as one example). Then, when you finally feel like you've nailed down a schedule and have clients committed to a time slot, there's the inevitable rescheduling! With group coaching, YOU set the day and time and if someone misses it, there is no rescheduling!
- Added accountability for participants—not simply committing to

themselves and YOU, they're publicly declaring their intentions and commitments!

- Added value for participants by having access to the collective wisdom and insight of the group, including feedback, networking, insight, and brainstorming.
- Running a group is fun, rewarding, and exciting!

THE WHAT OF YOUR GROUP COACHING BUSINESS

So, now that you've clarified **why** you want to do group coaching, take it a step further and identify **what** you want it to look like. And before you begin building your group, it's important to clarify what's in it for YOU and what YOU want.

- What income do you want to make (annually)? (Go with whatever number comes to you.)
  - Based on your coaching rates, how many clients would you need to have (total sessions) per month?
- What difference do you want to make?
  - What topic areas are you passionate about coaching people on?
  - What types of people do you want to help?
- What schedule would you like to create?
  - What are your schedule needs (to fit around other responsibilities)?
  - How many hours do you want to (or can you) work per week/month?
  - Do you need a consistent/regular schedule?
  - Can it or would you want it to fluctuate during different times of the year (seasonal, taking time off, etc.)?

THE STRUCTURE OF YOUR GROUP COACHING BUSINESS

THE BASICS

Now that you know why you're doing this and what you're hoping to get out of it, we'll begin building your group structure, one piece at a time. **Keep in mind that we'll cover many of these topics in more detail later and that you may not be able to answer these questions right away, or your ideas may change.** You can always come back to this page later after you have a better idea of how you want to structure your group.

*Please note: the majority of this book discusses how to structure and run **Virtual** groups, although most of the processes and strategies also apply to in-person groups.*

Format:

- Will your meetings be in person, teleconference, webinar, hybrid?
- Not sure? Find out what your ideal participants want. Ask them! (Who can you ask?)
- Are your clients local or distant?

Group size: 2+ people is a group! Common small groups are 5 to 20. Large can be unlimited (normally up to 100). Small groups are great for high levels of engagement where you intimately coach each participant and they are working closely together. Larger groups are better for programs that are educational, where everyone is working on the same process or training and in which you do not need to engage directly with all participants. However, large groups can be split into smaller subgroups, so the sky is the limit.

- How many clients do you want to *reach*? (A handful of clients per year, hundreds, thousands?)
- What is your group minimum? Maximum?

Duration: How long will each group session be? Sessions are commonly 60 to 90 minutes (for virtual sessions). They can be longer, but only if absolutely necessary, as time commitment may be a deterrent to registration. In-person groups or workshops can be substantially longer for 1-day events. Important points to consider are:

- What is the goal of your group time—answering questions? Learning material? Group discussions?
- What do you need to cover in each session and how long would it take?

- How long will your group program be? 4–6 weeks? 8–10 weeks? 3–4 months? 6 to 12 months?
- What are the outcomes your group is working on and how long would it take for them to achieve those outcomes?
- How much material is being covered (if any)?
- How frequently will your group meet? Weekly? Monthly? Multiple times per week?

A rule of thumb is that short programs should meet more frequently (3 to 6 times/month) while long programs can meet less frequently (1 to 2 sessions per month). In some cases, you meet frequently in the beginning while working intensively on material and then taper off to monthly meetings for accountability. In-person programs could begin with a long initial workshop followed by occasional or regular groups.

HOMEWORK FOR YOUR GROUP PARTICIPANTS:

- What will your group participants work on **in-between** sessions?
- Will they have homework (if you're training them) that they'll need to complete prior to the next session?
- Will they be implementing any changes in their life or business? Reflecting on anything?

Make sure to consider this when planning your group and decide when in the session to discuss what participants should be doing before you meet again.

THE CONTENT OF YOUR GROUP COACHING BUSINESS

OPEN COACHING VS. STRUCTURED PROGRAM

One of the biggest questions is… How much content should you include? There is no rule of thumb here. Here are some basic questions to help you consider what your group content may look like:

- Do you see group coaching as an extension of individual coaching, in which you coach several people simultaneously?

- Would your group participants each be setting their own, individual goals for the program and then working independently with both you and the other group members as support?

- Do you have expertise or a skill or program that you would want to teach or train about so that your participants could achieve a specific objective or implement this information during the group coaching session?

- Would you WANT to teach a structured program and teach the material to your coaching group? (Even if you don't already have something.)

Answering "yes" to the first two questions means you may be looking to run what we refer to as an *open coaching* group, while answering "yes" to the last two questions would imply you may be looking to create a *structured program*.

Open Coaching: The *content* in an open coaching group is determined by the individuals and the group. This is much like general coaching, in which you coach each individual as they work toward outcomes and goals that they set for themselves. Some of the features of Open Coaching are:

- In a group setting, you guide participants to determine the goals they have for their time in the group program and in what way the group can help them. *They* set the agenda (with your guidance), both for the group itself and the sessions.

- A major role as a coach in an open group is accountability. Participants also have the added accountability of the group members. The group members can also play a more active supportive role by providing feedback during sessions, as well as connecting and collaborating outside of group time.

- The group also sets goals, together, and determines how best to help everyone involved reach their individual goals.

- Often, open coaching groups are used to coach a small group of individuals who have *similar* goals (change careers, lose weight, stop a habit, etc.). Although you may not be focused heavily on teaching any specific strategies or tools, you may offer expertise or guidance in a particular area.

- Very often, open coaching groups are used when working with individuals who are already advanced in their skills.

Structured Program: The *content* in a structured program is the main purpose of the group. The primary reason participants join the group is because they want to learn or implement the training being provided during the program. Some of the features of Structured Program are:

- The entire group works on the same goals (usually at the same pace) through a concrete, structured, step-by-step program designed to achieve specific results.

- The coach plays the role of support and facilitation of the group *and* being a subject matter expert who is teaching the material to the group or training them.

- Participants also benefit from the wisdom, experience, and support of the other participants. Groups can be designed with a high level of engagement, in which participants mastermind with each other during group sessions (sharing intimately in small groups) and/or connecting with each other outside of the sessions. Groups can also be designed with a low level of engagement, in which the main focus of group sessions is to cover the material being learned.

- You don't have to have content that's already developed! You can create a program based on the material you already know, your expertise, or what you already coach about. Or, you can create a program based on someone else's material, such as a book. (Yes, you can do that! More on this later.)

- Masterminding is when participants not only encourage and support each other, they also collaborate by offering their individual expertise, and in some cases, literally work together.

- Number of participants: When conducting a structured program (specific outcomes, entire group following along), it is possible to facilitate very large groups. If operating a large group, in some cases, it may be possible or advisable to create smaller teams within the group in order to create that personal feel and the benefit of networking. For open coaching groups, small groups are necessary because the whole point is to be able to create intimate, supportive relationships with a small group of people. The ideal number is 3–5 and 10–20 is the maximum. Small groups are also more valuable (for either type of group) and you can charge more for them.

AN EXAMPLE OF A SMALL OPEN COACHING GROUP:

A Mini Mastermind

Rather than setting specific goals, I wanted to make it possible to work on what you need most in your life + business each week.

I also wanted you to be a part of something special + gain connections with like-minded women along the way.

Picture this: 2 other amazing, passionate and like-minded women + me all supporting you + helping you to bring your business vision to life or take the next steps toward your dreams.

What you will receive:

- 8 weeks of connection + direct attention to your life + business needs.
- A platform to brainstorm your ideas, ask questions + be coached through your challenges or blocks.
- Have a team of cheerleaders who believe in you and want you to succeed.
- Meeting online once a week for 90 minutes, email support in between sessions.
- Your own private Facebook Group.
- 1 x 30 minute follow up 1:1 session with me.

Are you ready to change the way you show up in your life plus build your business?

There are spaces for 3 big-dreaming, creative, spirited leaders to be a part of the next Solopreneurs Unite mini mastermind with me…

Your investment: $399 for the entire 8 weeks.

AN EXAMPLE OF A STRUCTURED PROGRAM:

(This could be operated as a large group because there is not as much engagement, or it could be offered in smaller groups with higher engagement.)

The Women Who Soar program includes:

One 60-minute group coaching session each month. These sessions are a combination of Q&A and coaching and are conducted by phone, so you can participate by calling from anywhere. I will provide you with a recording after each call. This allows you to listen as much and as often as you like to deepen your learning and understanding, even if you miss the live call.

- 10 podcasts over six months that include valuable information and success handouts designed to help overcome obstacles and move you forward. Topics include:
  - Create Your Vision
  - Regain Peace and Balance
  - Calm the Chaos
  - Discover Your Passion, Values, and Priorities
  - Awaken Your Intuition
  - Make More Empowered Choices
  - Stress Less and Thrive More
- Membership in the Women Who Soar private online discussion board.
- Subscription to Wings of Inspiration, the Monarch Leadership newsletter dedicated to addressing the current issues and challenges facing women in business.
- My full commitment and support in helping you achieve your goals and dreams.

When you sign up, you will receive your first podcast right away. Let the journey begin!

Your Investment:

I am offering two options for you to invest in yourself.

Women Who Soar: Group Coaching Package (a $600 value)

1. 1. Special package price: $85 per month for 6 months (total = $510)
2. 2. Paid in full up front: $459 (savings of 10% = $51)

THE PRICING OF YOUR GROUP COACHING BUSINESS

You need to consider a number of factors before setting the prices of your coaching group. We'll cover some basic guidelines. However, ultimately, it's up to you what to charge. We'll also look at some example numbers so you can clearly see both the options and the benefits of group coaching (that it can be extremely profitable!).

We will then look at the industry's most common group **coaching models** and how they are commonly priced.

- You must consider your market (what they can afford and what it's worth to them). What's your *best guess* for how much they'd be willing to pay? Have you participated in any groups? What was the cost?

- You must consider your needs (how much *you* want/need to make and in how much time you have to make it in). You answered the *how much do you want to make* question previously.

- Consider how many groups you wish to run and how much time you could dedicate to it and divide it out (desired monthly income divided by number of hours group coaching = amount you wish to make per group).

- Consider how many people you would like to have in an average group and divide it out (desired per group session revenue divided by the number of participants = your group coaching fee). Just guess if you have to! The point here is to compare the price you listed above with this price.

When in doubt, one rule of thumb is to set group coaching fees at one-third to half of your private 1-on-1 coaching fee.

EXAMPLE NUMBERS TO HELP YOU ENVISION THE POSSIBILITIES

Imagine you wanted to make $4,000/month:

- Option 1: 10 **1-on-1 clients** each paying $400/month for 4 hours per month = $4,000/month, 40 hours

- Option 2: 20 **group clients** each paying $200/month = $4,000/month

- 4 small groups of 5, 4 hours per month each = 16 hours/month
- 1 large group, 4 hours per month = 4 hours/month

Imagine you want to create a 6-figure ($100,000) per year business instead? (That's $8,333/month.)

- Option 1: Increase the number of **1-on-1 clients** you have to 21. This would bring you $8,400 in 84 hours.
- Option 2: Increase the number of **group clients** you have to 42. This would bring you in $8,400/month.
  - Run 10 small groups (of about 5), 4 hours each = 40 hours/month
  - Run one large group = 4 hours/month
- Option 3: *Increase how much you charge* **1-on-1 clients**. Keep the original 10 clients but charge $840/month each ($210/hour), bringing in $8,400/month in 40 hours.
- Option 4: *Increase how much you charge* **group clients**. Keep 20 clients but charge $420/month each ($105/hour), bringing in $8,400/month in 16 hours (for 4 small groups) or 4 hours (for one large group).

You can play with these numbers and find what works for you. You can charge more or less per month. You can have more or less clients. You can include anywhere from 2 to 4 sessions per month in your fee. But, either way, you don't have to feel stuck trading your time for dollars. You can free up your schedule and make more money at the same time!

GROUP COACHING MODELS

5 WAYS TO STRUCTURE GROUP PROGRAMS AND EXAMPLE PRICING

Most group programs have a start and end date, meaning the entire group goes through the process at the same time. This serves two purposes: first is for marketing purposes, to encourage enrollment by a specific date. And the other is to keep the group focused on achieving outcomes or covering material in a timely manner.

5 POPULAR GROUP COACHING MODELS

Note: The first 3 Models discussed are the main focus of this book.

MODEL 1: QUICK AND EASY GROUP

Structure: 4–6 weeks. Weekly group sessions for 60–90 minutes. In person or virtual.

Content: Can be an Open Group (focused on individual goals and group support) or a Structured Program (focused on content delivery and training).

Size/Engagement: Size depends on the level of engagement. A low-engagement group with a structured program is common in this model and large groups work well. If a highly engaged group is your preference, a small group of 5–20 is ideal (although a larger group can work if it's structured and/or you break them into smaller groups).

Cost: Low/medium investment. $197–$997 are common price-points. Depends on the level of engagement and access to you. Entry-level program. Offers clients an affordable way to experience your coaching expertise.

Upsell: At the end of the program, participants are given the opportunity to make further progress by enrolling in a more advanced program, such as a coaching package, VIP day, or more advanced group program.

Example: Jumpstart Your Job Search Group Coaching Program. Investment of $297. Juicy bonus—a 1-on-1 session with the coach. Participants watch course videos and work on activities during the week and then come together for a simple Q&A once a week for an hour. Questions can either be asked live or questions previously submitted (through email) can be selected and answered by the coach (and can even be pre-recorded). At the end, a discounted career coaching or VIP coaching day is offered.

MODEL 2: GROUP BOOTCAMP OR TRAINING

Structure: 8–10 weeks. Weekly group sessions for 60–90 minutes. In person or virtual. The longer duration gives ample time for you to get to know the participants, for them to get results, and provides enough time to tackle a big problem and/or a big goal.

Content: Bootcamps and trainings are almost always offered as a structured program. You are providing training—a proven, step-by-step system. Can be an Open Group (focused on individual goals and group support) that is more highly engaged and meets for longer than a Quick and Easy Group.

Size/Engagement: In most cases, these groups are highly interactive. It's important to encourage group engagement and participant connection, as the challenges they face are greater and the commitment longer, so accountability is key. For this reason, they're often limited to 20 or fewer participants, so everyone can get the attention they deserve (although a larger group can work if it's structured and/or you break them into smaller groups).

Cost: Because you're getting to something BIGGER—it's worth more. $997–$1997.

Upsell: At the end of the program, participants are given the opportunity to take things further by enrolling in the exclusive Mastermind or Signature Program or work 1-on-1 with the coach.

Example: Rock Your Career Bootcamp. Investment of $1997. Bonuses include the Discover Your Purpose online course, the Rock the Interview online course, and a 1-on-1 session with the coach. Participants watch course videos and work on activities during the week. Also, they collaborate in structured and unstructured collaboration with other group members, including discussions, support and activities directed by the coach. There is also a component in which everyone comes together for a Q&A once a week for 90 minutes. Questions should be asked live or at least the meeting should be live and answers in-depth (which is why the 90-minute meeting is important). At the end, a signature program, mastermind, live event, or private career coaching is offered.

MODEL 3: MASTERMIND (SIGNATURE PROGRAM)

Structure: 6–12 months. Weekly group sessions for 90 minutes. High level of engagement between participants (usually fully engaged), sometimes within the sessions and always through an online forum (or even 1-on-1). Retreats, workshops, trainings, or other in-person events are usually included. Often, signature programs also include personalized, private interaction with you and/or other coaches. The participants are paying for *access* and customized attention.

Content: Participants are looking not only for support and progress but also for skill development. These programs are always highly engaged and both structured and open coaching. This means the entire group is following your signature program—the expertise that you are teaching—while at the same time setting their own individual goals for implementing change in their life (and often business).

Size: Group size should always be small, ideally 8–12. Groups can be large—50+. However, with the high level of engagement involved, you will likely need a team of coaches to pull off a large group.

Cost: You're a subject matter expert with significant experience and expertise and participants are benefiting from the social capital of the masterminding process. Participants are paying for access to you and others in the group, both of which are highly valuable. Prices can be $5k to $25k or more. Consider that the participants are interested in investing this much time and money ONLY because:

- They believe the mentor offers the expertise and experience they need.
- They believe the process will guide them to achieving their desired goals.
- They know the processes and systems they'll learn and receive will shorten their learning curve and they'll reach success sooner.
- They see the benefits of being part of a community of peers, masterminding with like-minded people, and having the opportunity for high-level collaboration (providing motivation, focus, accountability, coaching, feedback, staying on track, and modeling).

Upsell: At the end of the program, offer the participants the opportunity to take things further by enrolling in high-cost 1-on-1 coaching or an even higher level mastermind, that is even more exclusive. We've seen coaches charge as much as $100,000 per year for their highest level Mastermind.

An important note about *right fit*: It is *extremely* important to make sure your participants are the **right fit** for the group. There is a reason you take your prospects and clients on a long journey of getting to know you and trying out your products and services before you invite them to join your mastermind-level group. They may have arrived here through a series of steps, from a giveaway to a webinar and then your Model 1 group and then here.

During this time, they are learning about you and your program and by the time they sign up, they are sure it's what they want. Hopefully, you've also had time to get to know them and can determine if they're truly ready to commit to the process. In masterminds in which group members will be collaborating, it is important that they are a good fit for each other! They need to be coming from a similar place (such as all being managers, all being entrepreneurs, all being at-home mothers, etc.) and they need to each bring something to the table that benefits the group. If they're not well matched, the synergy of masterminding and the social capital cannot develop.

Example: Outstanding Women Entrepreneurs Who Own It Mastermind (OWN). Investment of $9997. 1-year program. Participants watch course videos that train and guide them toward desired outcomes, including advanced, detailed activities. They participate in online discussions with group participants, as well as mastermind in small groups (or with the whole group if it's small), including working on questions and problem solving, as directed by the coach, developing business relationships and helping each other with projects.

Live weekly calls for 90+ minutes include live Q&A and laser coaching, in which one participant is coached live and used as an example for other participants. Participants also receive all marketing templates and business documents needed to set up and market their business, 3+ 1-on-1 sessions with a coach, and 2 live events with expert speakers providing additional tools and insights. (Higher cost programs could even include VIP days with the head coach [you] and a 1-week retreat in a tropical destination.)

MODEL 4: ONGOING OR DROP-IN COACHING GROUP

An alternative to the time-framed group coaching models is to have an ongoing group. It could be an open group, more like a support group, in which case each individual is working on their own goals while seeking support. Or, it can be a structured program in which you support clients in implementing long-term training, business development, or life change.

Methods of operating ongoing groups:

- Monthly **group coaching calls** in which participants can "drop in" when they wish to.
- A **membership program** with continued access to materials, tools and community.

- An **online course** that walks participants through your structured program at their own pace, using video and worksheets.

In most cases, the downside is that it is hard to have group synergy when members are coming and going. Often, this model necessitates the need to keep adding new content.

If the participants in your ongoing group engage with each other and don't follow a specific curriculum that you have set, consider asking the group to come up with its own agenda. Give participants an opportunity to suggest what they feel would most benefit them and the group.

MODEL 5: TEAM COACHING

Team coaching is for corporate or executive coaches. Often, the group participants are enrolled in the coaching group by a team leader (manager, project lead, executive, etc.). Usually, the purpose of the group is to accomplish specific goals. The group may be structured, in which case you are delivering material that either you or the organization has developed (depending on whether you are being hired to coach as a consultant or simply a facilitator). However, there may be no training involved and the group may simply focus on specific outcomes. Examples of team coaching include:

- Sales teams
- Leadership teams
- Global work teams
- Project teams
- Employees in a small business
- Department teams.

CHAPTER 2: DESIGNING YOUR GROUP

THE CONTENT: DESIGNING YOUR CONTENT

BRAINSTORMING YOUR CONTENT

If you're leaning toward conducting structured groups, consider the following points as you begin putting together your material:

- What content will you teach?
- Do you already have structured content that you could easily convert into a group coaching program?
- If so, what is the topic?
- What is the most common need your prospects or clients share with you?
- If you don't already have a curriculum or program, what topic areas could you teach?
- What expertise do you have to offer?
- What can you do easily that others find difficult?
- What do you know how to do that others would PAY to learn a shortcut? What are you passionate about helping with?
- What do you currently focus on in your coaching (do you have a niche, such as career, health, happiness, etc.)?
- What material would you love to teach that someone else has developed, such as a methodology you love or even a book? (As long as you're clear where the material comes from, give credit

where it's due, and do not claim others' material as your own, this is a viable option.)

Important Tip: Before you put a great deal of time into developing a program based on the material you *think* people will want or need, do some research (or actually ask them). Often, coaches or teachers create programs *they* find interesting and then have no one sign up because they didn't take the time to determine what others wanted.

DESIGNING YOUR CONTENT

Decide what you want the group participants to learn. Determine if you need to measure participant learning. Then, plan visual materials, interactive elements, verbal lessons, quizzes, and assignments accordingly. Your primary aim is to deliver a transformative learning experience. For this to happen, your content needs to bring the participants to their desired future state. Hence, deliberate over the following questions and write out your answers in a separate sheet of paper. (You can later include the most important elements of your answers in the outline provided at the end of this chapter.)

- What is your process (for coaching and/or what you teach about)? What steps do you use to get results with your clients that you repeat with every client? *(This would be just like writing down the recipe for chocolate chip cookies. What are the ingredients, what steps do you take, what factors or tools do you need, etc.)*

- What are the different steps within this process and how could you break them down into material for different sessions? (Are there any processes within this process?)

- What makes *you* or *your process* different, better, more effective, etc.? (How do you differentiate yourself? What will attendees walk away with that they may not get anywhere else?)

- What are the *outcomes* the attendees will have or experience after attending your workshop?

INTRODUCING YOUR CONTENT

This material is great for use in your **first group session**, as well as in a **webinar** in which you're teaching one portion of your "process" and inviting them to join your group.

Goal of the introduction is to:

22

- position yourself as an expert
- let your audience know they're in the right place
- give them an overview of what they'll learn (that day and during the entire program)

Positioning Yourself:

Identify 3 Points of Credibility:

State your main vulnerability (your story):

"This is for you if…"

(Describe the traits of the participants that bring them to your workshop and describe what transformation they crave that you will offer (see the "outcomes" you determined above). This shows them you understand them and helps them have buy-in.)

"What you will learn…"

(This is where you tell the participants what you're going to tell them in this session and in the program. Fill this part in after finishing your outline.)

DESIGNING CONTENT FOR INTRODUCTORY WEBINARS

One great strategy for designing a webinar is using the introductory material above combined with 1 step in your process. This helps the participants to get to know you, shows them your expertise and gives them a taste of your program. Then, you offer them an incentive (an irresistible offer) to join your group at the end of the webinar.

We have a course called Get Life Coaching Clients with Workshops *that's designed to help you create an introductory presentation (such as a webinar) that informs attendees about your signature program (or group program) in a way that doesn't feel "salesy." It uses the outline above and walks you through completing the design for your program and more detail about the importance of each section.*

DESIGNING INDIVIDUAL SESSION MATERIAL

Review the process you identified above and the steps within the process. Determine what steps/topics you will cover in each weekly group coaching session (6 sessions? 10? 24+?).

Now, use the outline below for EACH step/session to design what material you will cover. Consult the lessons on Session Structure for implementing the coaching process with the content you are designing here.

Step/Topic for This Session:

- Focus/Title
- Est. Time (minutes)
- Summary and main points
- Supporting Examples (photos, videos, testimonials/case studies, examples, etc.)
- Interactive Activities
- Homework or Workbook Activities

SESSION STRUCTURE: DESIGN THE RECIPE OR FRAMEWORK THAT EACH SESSION FOLLOWS

Designing a group coaching program, and the structure of each individual session, is like creating your own recipe. We are providing you the ingredients here that are common in coaching sessions. It is up to you to determine which elements to combine in your very own recipe!

We provide a Session Template, which you can use to design each of your sessions, including the structure, elements, timing, and content.

Elements of a session which you can include based on your needs:

- **Laser check-in (all group members participate):** Example check-in topics include: most successful achievement since the last session, biggest challenge since the last session, main goal for this week, something they're grateful for, sharing of concerns, suggested question or topic for group discussion (if appropriate), etc. This is not recommended for large groups. It is very important to stay on top of timing for each participant. One way to do this is to ask that the check-in be one sentence.

- **Training or content delivery:** Presentation of material from your structured program.

- **Group discussion:** Sharing of ideas, insights and/or questions related to the structured content and/or personal or group goals.

- **Group Activity:** This can be an icebreaker, a warm-up or a process that is part of your structured program.

- **Live laser coaching:** This is the "hot seat" in which you coach an individual on their personal situation as a teaching moment for the entire group. (*See page 56.*)

- **Laser round table:** Like laser-coaching but done by the group. One participant shares a specific question or challenge they have and then each person in the group shares a key point, question, or wisdom about the scenario (ideally 30 seconds).

- **Action commitments:** Direct participants to decide what their next steps are and what action they will complete between now and the next session. Have them write this down. Depending on the group, you can have them share their commitment with the group for added accountability.

- **Laser takeaways:** Check-in with group members at the end of the session. (*See page 67.*)

Notice many of these started with the word LASER? Make sure to read the section about Laser Speak twice!

THE IMPORTANCE OF TIMING:

The amount of time you allot for each segment of your session depends completely on the type of group you are facilitating (open or structured) and the goals or outcome for your group.

If you're running an open group, you can allot a majority of your session time to various group discussions, check-ins, or round tables. With a highly engaged group, you can even allow them to determine the agenda for the session. (However, in most cases, group coaches have sessions planned long before the session happens.)

So always ask yourself: "What is the main goal or outcome for this session?" "What segments would add value to this session and which segments should be skipped this time (or every time)?" Then, allot your time accordingly.

If your group is primarily focused on structured content or training, do some practice runs with your material to see how long it takes you to present information. Then, when planning each session, you'll have a better idea of how much time to plan for each topic you discuss. Then, consider what elements of group participation would work well for your program and assign the remaining time to group sharing. As much as possible, minimize the time spent on group sharing, such as check-ins, takeaways, and group discussions. If you feel like discussions would be valuable, however, your training material will take the duration of the session. Three ways to engage the group better and answer questions are:

- Encourage participants to have conversations with each other through your group's discussion area (such as a Facebook group).

- Provide access to the ability to meet (including virtually) with each other in smaller groups to discuss material or mastermind together outside of session time.

- Encourage participants to submit questions to you via email, which you can either answer directly or answer during live sessions focused on Q&A. (Alternatively, you can hold a session dedicated to answering questions *live*.)

Note: If you plan to answer personal questions as part of your coaching program, consider the added time this will take you (based on the number of participants) when determining how much to charge for your group. Also, be sure to include email limits in your guidelines or agreement.

Be aware that it is highly likely your group discussions will take longer than expected. Even simple check-ins can get out of hand if you are not extremely clear about the expectations for laser speak or a time limit and/or are not vigilant about enforcing these limits. *Always overestimate the amount of time it will take for group activities.*

Consider planning group discussion or questions for the end of the session. This way, should your session go over the scheduled time period, you can let group members know that they can choose to stay on the call (or at the meeting) longer if they wish. Doing this ensures you cover the agenda for the day and that people with time constraints do not miss out on vital information.

Use the content you designed in the *Designing Your Content* section to complete this outline (next page) and schedule for each session. Simply create one sheet for each of your group coaching meetings.

THE FIRST SESSION

You've already looked at the structure of a session and the different elements that you can include in each session. However, the first session has different needs, and therefore, it has a different structure.

It's important to start the first session *strong*. It's your opportunity to lay the foundation, set expectations, and gain group buy-in. You want to get participants excited and give an opportunity for them to get to know you and each other (if appropriate).

Common elements of a first session include the following:

Laser Introductions: If your group will be engaging at any level, it may be a good idea for each participant to briefly introduce themselves. Remind participants to use laser speak and consider narrowing the scope of the introduction to name, location, what they "do" and/or 1-sentence goal for participating in the group, or something similar. If learning each others' names is of benefit to the group, consider an activity such as "Color My Name."Ask participants to select a color and introduce themselves as that color and their name "Blue Molly James" followed with a brief explanation about why they chose that color. For example: "I am Blue Molly James and I am blue like the ocean—deep, cool and always in motion and connecting everything!"

SESSION FOCUS (or content title):	Y/N	Time
Desired goals and outcomes:		
Check-in or warm-up:		
Agenda, summary, points to cover, and/or examples:		
Activities or group discussions:		
Laser coaching or round table:		
Takeaways/Group closure:		
Homework or action commitments:		
Other resources needed:		

Ice Breakers/Group Activity: Take introductions to another level with an extended group activity that *breaks the ice*, helps participants get to know each other, forms social bonds, and opens up communication.

Ground Rules: Going over the ground rules is the #1 most important part of the first session. This is your opportunity to set expectations for the rest of the group program. At the minimum, the following **5 Key Expectations** must be addressed. (*See the Ground Rules section in this chapter for important considerations and other ideas.*)

- Attendance
- Active Listening
- Laser Speak
- Confidentiality
- Respect.

Training or content delivery: Determine what material from your structured program you would like to cover in your first session. Usually, this is your introductory material. The 3 main parts of your introduction should include:

- Introduce yourself (your expertise, your story, etc.)
- Let your audience know they're in the right place
- Give them an overview of what they'll learn.

Outline and Overview: At the minimum, you need to go over the outline for the program, how it will work, and an overview of what they will be learning. This includes:

- The schedule, duration, length of sessions
- Group structure (how meeting, level of engagement)
- Roles and expectations for the participants and the coach
- Homework and in-between session expectations
- The outline of the program and topics covered during each week.

Group Discussion: Conduct a group discussion. There are two topics that are a great way to begin your groups by discussing during the first session:

- ***Group Mission Statement:*** It creates buy-in and inspires and motivates group members to stay focused and check in regularly to evaluate if they are "on mission." **The #1 mistake many**

coaches make is not ensuring the group has consensus regarding the outcomes they are seeking from the group. We discuss this in more detail in the *Fully Engaged Groups* section in this chapter.

- *Group Agenda and Goals:* To the degree it is appropriate for the type of group you are running, the participants can work together to set an agenda and/or set goals for the group. In the *Ground Rules* section, we discuss how asking group members for input regarding what rules will make the group experience better for all involved. In the same way, having them set goals and agendas together, even if it's simply going over what the agenda and goals are (if they're pre-established) and asking for input, gives participants more *buy-in.*

Commitment: There are many ways you can ask group members to commit to the group process and what you choose will depend on the type of group you run. Participants can make commitments by writing in a journal or course material and/or you can ask them to share with the group. Forms of commitment that can be discussed include:

- Committing to themselves to be dedicated to their goals and to complete the program
- Committing to the group to contribute, show up, and complete the program
- Committing to specific actions they will take before the next group session.

CONFIDENTIALITY AND TRUST

Developing trust—Trust in a group comes down to two essential attributes: confidentiality and respect. With regard to respect, each participant must feel that the members of the group will not pass judgment on them or treat them unkindly.

Establish the expectation that all members of the group will honor each other by valuing their privacy as well as their choices. This means it is not any participant's role to agree or disagree with another participant or to judge his or her beliefs or decisions. Establishing this helps ensure the group does not feel it needs to gain consensus on any topics or reject others for differing views. While the group is working collectively, ultimately the purpose of group coaching is for the development of the individual in whatever way suits him or her best.

FIRST SESSION TEMPLATE

THE FIRST SESSION	Y/N	Time
Laser Introductions		
Ice Breaker		
Ground Rules • Attendance • Active Listening • Laser Speak • Confidentiality • Respect		
Training/Content/Introduction		
Outline and Overview • The schedule, duration, length of sessions • Group structure (how meeting, level of engagement) • Roles and expectations for the participants and the coach • Homework and in-between session expectations • The outline of the program and topics covered during each week		
Group Discussion (Mission, Agenda, Goals, Other)		
Commitment		
Other resources needed:		

Why trust matters—When trust is established, participants will feel comfortable being vulnerable and honest in the group, without censoring their circumstances. This can lead to important breakthroughs, as participants allow themselves to open to deeper levels of transformation, while feeling supported by the group.

Pledge of Confidentiality—Ask group members to make a pledge of confidentiality. This is usually in writing and includes agreeing not to share audio recordings or personal observations or information about others. You can include it in the Ground Rules and/or ask them to recite a pledge in the first session.

Discussing Confidentiality—Ask the group to brainstorm what it would take to create an environment of trust and confidentiality, as it may mean different things to different people and, more importantly, if they collectively develop the rules (or add to them) they will have more buy-in to following them.

GROUND RULES

Ground rules should be developed and adapted for every unique context. Appropriate ground rules may depend partially on the type or topic of your group, age, region, and other contextual factors.

TIPS FOR DEVELOPING GROUND RULES:

1. Start with basic ground rules to set a foundation and minimize having to create them after something comes up.

2. Spend about 5 to 10 minutes in the first session going over the rules and getting feedback.

3. Get the group involved: Ask the group if they would like to add any rules to what has been established.

4. As much as possible, avoid making new ground rules during a session if an issue arises.

5. Get **buy-in** by letting the group know that it is up to all of us to hold each other accountable for maintaining the rules.

6. Remember that rules are not laws. They are guidelines to help make the group thrive and not create as a punishment. Therefore, be flexible when

developing them. Use them as an opportunity to help people grow.

7. If the group meets in person, have the rules posted in a visible place so that they can serve as a reminder. If the meeting is virtual, include ground rules in your pre-group agreement and have each participant sign or acknowledge the rules prior to the first group meeting.

SAMPLE GROUND RULES

Attendance: I will arrive at the coaching group on time and be ready to being at the designated time.

Active Listening: I will give whoever is speaking my full attention and listen not only to their words but to the deeper meaning behind them. (See *Active Listening* section in Chapter 4.)

"I" Statements: Speak from your own experience instead of generalizing ("I" instead of "they," "we," and "you").

Laser Speak: I will respect group time by using clear and concise language and avoid long, detail-oriented stories or explanations.

Confidentiality: I will maintain complete confidentiality about anything that another participant shares during the coaching group. This includes agreeing not to share audio recordings.

Support: I will encourage and support my fellow group members through championing their success contributing in whatever way that I can.

Participation: I will make participation in the group a high priority, including contributing to group discussions and supporting group members. Community growth depends on the inclusion of every individual voice.

Distractions: I will be fully present for each group session and will not multi-task. I will also turn off my cell phone and other devices and minimize other people being around me.

Accountability: I will hold myself accountable to commitments I make to myself and the group, as well as hold other participants accountable through positive peer support and encouragement.

Feedback: I will provide positive feedback and will provide appropriate negative feedback only if asked.

Respect: I will treat all group members with respect and courtesy, including honoring each participant's unique viewpoints, beliefs and needs. The goal is not to agree—it is to gain a deeper understanding. Do not be afraid to respectfully challenge one another by asking questions but refrain from personal attacks—focus on ideas. Be conscious of your body language and nonverbal responses—they can be as disrespectful as words.

Interrupting: I will refrain from interrupting others as they speak.

Grievances: I will communicate any grievances immediately and directly with the coach.

FULLY ENGAGED GROUPS

We've discussed two different types of groups: open groups and structured groups. While structured groups focus more on content and training, open groups are more like individual coaching, which is directed by the goals of the client, however in a group setting. It's extremely important for your open groups to be fully engaged.

Of course, you can create fully engaged groups in any structure and with any model. The important thing to know is whether it is appropriate for the type of group you are running. In some cases, especially a program heavily focused on training (like a Bootcamp) or one that doesn't last very long, fully engaging a group can be a distraction to your goals.

Fully Engaged: When a group is fully engaged, the participants:

- Can connect to and relate to each other through commonalities (which is why it's important to have groups in which clients share a common career, experience, or goal)
- Participate actively in the group (and collaborate when appropriate)
- Take it a step further and **contribute** to the group—reciprocity.

It creates enthusiasm and accountability, which is the ideal environment for goal achievement to happen. Involvement becomes irresistible and attracts typically *side sitting* group members to participate.

Social Capital: Focus on building social capital in fully engaged groups (and especially Masterminds). Social capital goes beyond simply networking. Networking and less engaged group experiences usually focus on what each participant can *get* out of the experience and/or from other participants. When relationships are reciprocal and embody the principle of giving and receiving, social capital is developed.

As the coach, your role is to encourage this key ingredient of reciprocity by asking participants to determine what they bring to the table—what value they can offer the group. You will find that they are eager to contribute because they love to help! This is a huge benefit to participants, and through online collaboration, participants gain access to like-minded peers from around the globe, whom they would otherwise not have access to.

Group Mission Statement: In order to have full engagement, the participants in the group must be very clear about the group's overall goal. For this reason, creating a group mission statement is essential. It creates buy-in and inspires and motivates group members to stay focused and check in regularly to evaluate if they are *on mission*. A good mission statement should be:

- Inspiring and exciting
- Clear and outcome focused
- No longer than one sentence
- Recited by memory easily.

Non-Coach Engagement: A powerful element that can be added to fully engaged groups is to encourage collaboration *without* the coach. In all groups, having participants connect through a forum where they can share ideas and get to know each other is an important component. However, in a fully engaged group, it can further bond the group by holding occasional meetings in which the group meets *without* the coach being present. In this case, the group determines the agenda. They can also use this time to elaborate on topics, details or stories that regular sessions don't allow time for (due to the focus on laser speak).

GROUP STAGES

One thing that we have learned from the variety of groups we have worked with is that regardless of the structure, the purpose, population, and setting, all groups go through similar stages. As a coach who is looking to incorporate group coaching as part of their practice, it is important to understand that there are unique tools that you need to acquire to truly be able to facilitate and develop group dynamics that will help the group achieve their goals.

The higher the level of engagement your group has, the more these group stages will be relevant. A structured group almost entirely focused on content with very little interaction, on the other hand, will not display these stages in the same way.

Knowing what to expect and planning for it will make sure you're prepared and everything goes smoothly. We will address the phases that you may experience when working with your groups. This model we describe was created by Psychologist Bruce Tuckman. He first came up with it in 1965 and has continued to adapt and develop it throughout the years, going from four phases to five: forming, storming, norming, performing, and adjourning.

This model is one of the most widely used models in the field of coaching. Don't worry. We will explain it in a way that is easy to digest to help you understand what it means to you and to the groups that you will serve. We will break down each phase into feelings, behaviors, and tasks.

You can use the stages and steps below to ensure that you are helping the group continue to move forward.

- Make sure to identify the stage of group development that your group is in.
- Adjust your behavior and leadership approach appropriately throughout your program.

STAGE 1: FORMING

In the beginning, as a coach, you will play a critical and dominant role as team members will look at you to understand their roles and responsibilities in this process. This stage can last beyond the first session as people get more comfortable in their expectations and get to know each other at a deeper level.

Feelings: This is the first stage of group dynamics. It is that stage in which everyone seems to be positive and polite with each other. As any new experience that may be life changing, you will have a variety of emotions within the group. Some people may feel a little uncomfortable and anxious, while others will be excited. This is because they do not fully understand what the group will entail, how they will connect to others, and what will happen.

Behaviors: In this phase, the behaviors of individuals will be driven by curiosity and a need to connect to the group. Therefore, the partici-

36

pants may ask a lot of questions that reflect their excitement and their need to know more and connect with other members of the group.

Tasks: The main role during the forming stage is to create a clear structure, goals, direction, and roles so that each member begins to build trust and feel more comfortable with the process and environment. An overview of what they can expect along with an opportunity for people to get to know you as a coach, as well as each other, is a great way to start developing bonds that will help the group grow and develop. The majority of the time spent during this phase may be toward laying a solid foundation and developing connections within the team.

Tips: Direct the group and establish clear objectives, both for the team as a whole and for each individual.

STAGE 2: STORMING

The next phase may be challenging for some coaches if they are not prepared or do not expect to deal with this transition. As a group facilitator, expecting this stage makes it easier to know what to do and not to personalize it or see it as a reflection of you. In this phase, people start pushing against boundaries, showing resistance, and displaying more of the patterns that may be holding them back in their life or business. Many times, an inability to truly transition from this phase can hold the group back from creating an environment of support and transformation.

This phase may start when group members' temperaments, personalities, or communication styles become incompatible with other members of the group. Everyone in the group may have different expectations, different needs, or different ways of approaching situations, which can lead to frustration. This stage may also come about when a group member challenges your authority or tries to exert their own control of the group. For some people, having a sense of control may be a pattern in their life. Some may also question the purpose of certain activities as they may start experiencing resistance to change.

Feelings: As the group starts to move toward its goals, clients may question whether the group can live up to all of their expectations and their initial excitement. Therefore, they may shift the positive emotions toward frustration or anger with the team's progress or process. During this stage, members are assessing how the group responds to differences and how it will handle conflict.

Behaviors: During this stage, participants may be less polite than during the initial phase. Some frustration or disagreements may be openly expressed. This frustration may be directed toward other participants, the group process, and/or the facilitator.

Tasks: During this stage, it is important to refocus and clarify group and individual goals as it can help get members past frustration and confusion. People like to be reassured that they are on the right path with the right people. It may also be necessary to break larger goals down into smaller, achievable steps. It is important for the facilitator to assess if the group can benefit from developing task-related skills and conflict management skills. For example, working on communication skills and demonstrating how what is learned in the group will also be applicable in other relationships and situation that they may experience outside of the group.

Tips:

- Establish or reinforce the group processes and structures.

- Make sure to do activities that build trust and good relationships between group members.

- If conflicts arise, do not let them get out of hand. Make sure that conflicts are resolved promptly if they occur. Remember, you are setting a foundation of what is acceptable. Provide support, especially for those group members who may feel less secure.

- During this transition, make sure to remain positive but at the same time, be firm in dealing with challenges concerning the group norms, your leadership, or the group's goals.

- Explain that it is normal and healthy for groups to go through this phase, and that it will only help the group become stronger and more united in working towards their goals. This will help the group see that it will get better in the future and develop an understanding of why the problem is occurring.

- In team groups, consider using psychometric indicators such as the Myers Briggs Type Inventory (Personality) so that people can better understand each other.

STAGE 3: NORMING

The group will gradually move toward the norming stage. In this phase, group members will solve conflicts and come to appreciate the differences in the group, and develop respect and trust with the group and the leader. Depending on the group, there may be some overlap between storming and norming as new tasks, goals, and challenges come up in the group.

Feelings: If the group is successful at navigating out of the storming phase, they will develop an increased sense of trust and comfort in fully expressing ideas and feelings. There will be a feeling of acceptance of others and a recognition that the variation of perspective and experience makes the group stronger. At this point, constructive criticism is both possible and welcomed. Individuals in the group start to truly feel that they are part of a community and find pleasure in being part of the group.

Behaviors: In this phase, you may notice that group members make a conscious effort to resolve problems to achieve group harmony. Since the group has a deeper connection and has developed more trust, you should see more meaningful communication, an increased willingness to be open about feelings and ideas, and also more openness to asking group members for help. The group may start developing inside jokes and a deeper understanding of other's needs.

Tasks: During this stage, the group should be more productive both in individual goals and collective group goals. This is a great time to help the group and individual members reflect and evaluate what they are working on and the process.

Tips:
- This is a great time to step back and help individuals and group members to take responsibility for their progress toward the goal.
- It may be a great time to create accountability partners.

STAGE 4: PERFORMING

When the group reaches this stage, they may start feeling a sense of accomplishment for the transformation that has happened in them as individuals and as a group. The group leader can delegate some roles and help empower the group members.

Feelings: In this stage, group members may experience satisfaction with their own progress, as well as the group's progress. Many in the group will have an understanding of their strength and weakness and those of the group. Group members feel attached to the group and feel confident in their individual abilities and those of the group members to reach individual goals and group goals.

Behaviors: The group members are empowered to prevent or solve challenges in the process. You will notice that there may be an "I/we can do it" attitude. Group members are also more empowered to make bigger changes in their transformation process with less fear of change.

Tasks: In this phase, group members make significant progress toward their own goals. You will see more commitment to the process and in embracing the learning process to acquire more knowledge and skills that will help them achieve their goals. It is important to help champion and celebrate the progress that has been achieved.

Tips:

- Continue to step back and empower members to hold each other accountable and to coach themselves and make bigger leaps toward their own transformation.
- Celebrate and remind people how far they have come.
- Keep in mind that changes, such as members coming or going or other major changes, can lead the group to revert back to an earlier stage. However, if the changes are addressed properly, the group can successfully remain in this stage indefinitely.

STAGE 5: ADJOURNING

Every process may have a termination day. This is the final stage, when the group is coming to a close.

Feelings: This can be more difficult than some coaches would imagine. In fact, some group members may experience mixed emotions and even a sense of loss. This is especially true for those who like routines and consistency. Therefore, they may experience anxiety and/or sadness. This can be true for the group members and the facilitators alike. At the same time, they may cycle through positive and negative emotions. Of course, the more highly engaged your group is, the more the ending of the group will affect group members.

Behaviors: During this stage, some members may be less focused and their motivation to work on their final goals may decrease. Some may not even want to attend the last couple of meetings as a defense mechanism of not having to deal with the emotions.

Tasks and Tips: It is important for the group to acknowledge and deal with the upcoming transition and the feelings that are attached to them. Some steps that you can take to help the process are:

- Be preventive and start the discussion of the group's closure a couple of meetings before the last one so that the group members can start processing the closure.

- Evaluate any activities that need to be completed before the group reaches the last meeting.

- Create a closing celebration that provides closure. This celebration should acknowledge the contributions of individuals to the group and their accomplishment in this process. The celebration can include the participants preparing a statement for the group and a commitment that they are making to themselves moving forward.

- Provide resources and a way that the group members can continue the process on their own, work with you as a coach, or even stay in contact with each other if they choose.

GROW AND GROUP COACHING METHODOLOGIES

THE GROW MODEL

Grow model is a popular model to use for coaching including group coaching. *This is specifically useful if you're running an OPEN coaching group.*

GROW stands for Goal, Reality, Options, Way Forward. Let's examine the four steps more closely.

Step 1: GOAL: Participants set a goal for the session and/or the week. This can be individual goals and/or group goals.

Questions:

- What do you want to achieve in this session?
- What about between now and the next session?
- What's the best use of this time?

Step 2: REALITY: Group members explore the *current reality* as it relates to their goals.

Questions:

- How have you handled any challenges this week?
- What worked and what didn't?

Step 3: OPTIONS: Brainstorm and explore options for action.

Questions:

- What possible options do you have?
- What has worked in the past?
- What haven't you tried yet?

Step 4: WAY FORWARD: Determine next steps and develop action plans.

Questions:

- What is the most important action you need to take next?
- What might get in the way?
- Who will be able to support you?
- How will you feel when this is done?

Conversations can be directed using this list of questions. During the sessions, you may need to go back and forth between checking in with the current reality, reassessing goals, and determining options and steps. However, always make sure to finish the session with clearly defined goals and action steps to be able to complete before the group meets again.

Each subsequent coaching session begins by having members review and evaluate the goals from the previous session. You can take this time to assess what went right and if any challenges prevented them from achieving their goals. This is also a good time to champion group members. Afterward, the cycle will repeat, and the participants will set new goals for the next session.

Of course, the GROW model can be used for group coaching as well as one-on-one coaching. However, an important facet of group coaching is group dynamics, which the GROW model doesn't cover. Next, we'll talk about the GROUP coaching model that expands on the GROW model, making it more practical for working with a group.

THE GROUP MODEL

GROUP stands for Goal, Reality, Options, Understanding Others, Perform. This model follows the same initial 3 steps of the GROW Model of goal setting, reality exploration and option generation. Where these two models differ are in the fourth stage (the *Understanding Others* step). When working in groups, one of the biggest key to success is the ability to truly understand others. A group can only go as far as the dynamics of the group allow through mutual understanding and support.

Depending on the way you are running your group, you can have each participant share during each step in the model or if time doesn't permit this, you can have different participants share at different times, and your discussion with the individual will serve as an example for the group.

Use the first 3 steps from the GROW Model. Let's look at the last two steps.

Step 4: UNDERSTANDING OTHERS: The members of the group observe deeply, have open conversations, and become aware of their internal responses.

Questions:

- What did you understand about her view?
- What was your internal dialog while you were listening to that?

This step is designed to foster open conversations, allowing individuals to receive feedback, share experiences, and explore possible blind spots that may hold them back from achieving their desired goals. If the group has trust and understanding, they will be genuinely open to possibilities and can let go of the human need for certainty and the need to be right.

The role of the coach in the *Understanding Others* step is to help group members be able to suspend judgment, become comfortable with uncertainty and ambiguity, be open to listen to other group members, and be able to listen to their own personal internal processes. To be successful in developing this type of community, it is important that, as a coach, you encourage participants to question their own assumptions—beyond just actively listening—because it will open the door for true genuinely listening. Without their biases and opinions distracting them from what is being said, they'll better be able to understand others and come up with options.

Again, you may not have time for the group to have a discussion about each member's goals and possibilities. However, you can use a roundtable or select discussions, seeking feedback from the whole group or select members.

Step 5: PERFORM: Develop individual and group action plans and ensure accountability.

Questions:

- What is the most important thing to do next?
- What might get in the way?
- Who will be able to support you?
- How will you feel when this is done?

In the final step, the group transitions from option generation and dialogue and into developing action plans and strategies. Sharing individual goals with the group ensures clarity, transparency, commitment, and accountability for all group members.

During this step (throughout the group program), group members question their own assumptions, try new things, and receive feedback. This process allows the person to come up with creative ideas. (This type of learning is called double-loop learning in psychology.)

Problems and challenges that clients face cannot be solved with the same level of thinking that created them. When participants can develop confidence in themselves and view challenges as opportunities to grow and develop, it transforms their ability to succeed in any aspect of their life. This comes from the willingness to fail, be vulnerable, and embrace uncertainty in life.

RE-GROUP: The Review and Evaluate Step

With each GROUP coaching session, the idea development and refinement continues following a process of RE-GROUP (Review, Evaluate, Goal, Reality, Options, Understand Others, Perform). Therefore, the action steps and goals that were determined in the previous session are systematically reviewed and evaluated before any new goals are established.

- REVIEW: Assess the action steps taken since the last meeting and some of the challenges.

- EVALUATE: Examine underlying assumptions of the situation. Many times, when the participant is able to reframe the problem and see it from a different perspective, they are able to come up with new ideas and solutions. Also, the solution to any problem comes from asking the right questions. When the group and the coach ask questions and give feedback, individuals may be able to create different approaches to their situation.

POINTS TO KEEP IN MIND

One of the most important points to remember when conducting coaching and group coaching is that any methodology that is utilized must be flexible and client-centered. It's important for the coach to recognize whether they are meeting the needs of the participants.

For example, some groups may benefit more from having the *Understanding* step before the *Option* step. This can be in situations where members have a limited or low understanding of each other's needs, strengths, and resources. And this information may benefit the group before moving forward to exploring the options that a person may have.

How to use a methodology like the GROUP Model truly depends on the group and level of engagement that the group will have. In other cases, you may find that the group has challenges coming up with specific goals at the beginning of the coaching session. In this situation, the group may benefit from first exploring the *Reality* step before moving on to goal setting.

In other words, it is more important for the coach to be open to the group's needs rather than just force a specific process or model of coaching. Therefore, the GROUP model is more of a foundation, a mental model, rather than a strict step-by-step process.

TECHNOLOGY NEEDED FOR COACHING GROUPS

The entire process of creating and running a coaching group will require several forms of technology. There are ways you can operate groups very "low-tech." However, the added efficiency and functionality of using technology far outweighs the costs. For in-person groups, minimal technology is needed. However, all areas below must still be addressed.

FUNCTIONS IN NEED OF TECHNOLOGY FOR GROUP COACHING:

- Register participants and collect payment
- Video or teleconference service or in-person meeting place
- Communicate with your participants and prospects (email)
- Enable participants to connect with each other
- Content delivery system

1) REGISTER PARTICIPANTS AND COLLECT PAYMENT

In person—cash, check, credit card. If you want to accept a credit card, two great services which you can use through your phone or tablet/iPad are Square or PayPal. Get a free card swiper that plugs into your phone and set up a free account. Normal credit card processing fees apply.

On business website—Accept credit card payments for registration through your website.

- PayPal button directly in your website (https://www.paypal.com/webapps/mpp/get-started/buy-now-button)
- WordPress shopping cart plugin (http://www.wpeasycart.com) Other options available.
- WordPress PayPal shopping cart plugin (https://wordpress.org/plugins/wordpress-simple-paypal-shopping-cart/) Other options available.
- Wix.com shopping cart (https://www.wix.com/support/html5/article/adding-a-shopping-cart)

2) VIDEO OR TELECONFERENCE SERVICE OR IN-PERSON MEETING PLACE

In-person—Good locations to hold coaching groups include: corporate offices, libraries, community centers, bookstores, spiritual centers, even private homes. Some locations may offer free space. However, in most cases, you will pay a fee to rent space.

Teleseminars—Teleseminars are phone and web-based meetings in which participants join by calling in or listening online. Some teleseminar platforms offer advanced features, including breaking callers into smaller groups. Pricing is determined based on the number of participants you wish to have and what features you select. Which one works best for you is based on how interactive you need your group to be, whether you have multiple presenters, and how many participants you have.

If live video is important for your meetings, a webinar service may be better. However, alternatives exist for occasional video, such as Facebook live. Also, some teleseminar platforms include video options.

BASIC FEATURES:

- Host phone controls and online dashboard
- Mute/unmute
- Ability for participants to "raise their hand"
- Chat function
- Conference recording
- Access to download recordings
- Replay page where attendees can listen to the call after the live event is over.

ADVANCED FEATURES:

- Customizable broadcast page
- Pre-recorded audio plays as live
- Calls-to-action that bring participants to your sign-up page
- Q&A submission on broadcast page

- Breakout groups
- Identify callers by name
- Polling
- Webinar functionality (video)
- Screen sharing
- Registration and payments accepted directly in the broadcast page.

3 EXAMPLE PLATFORMS

- Basic: http://www.freeconferencecalling.com
- Normal: http://instantteleseminar.com
- Advanced: http://maestroconference.com

WEBINARS

Webinars operate similar to teleseminars. However, the focus is on video. Also, while in a teleseminar, ALL participants can participate in the conversation. However, in a webinar, a limited number of people can participate via video. The rest are simply watching. Some platforms offer both teleseminar and webinar functionality. Some require downloading and installing a computer-based system, others are web based.

Pricing is determined based on the number of participants you wish to have and what features you select. Which one works best for you is based on how interactive you need your group to be, whether you have multiple presenters, and the number of participants in your group.

BASIC FEATURES:

- Live video broadcasting
- Multi-presenter (or participant) video feeds (2 to 10)
- Screensharing and Powerpoint
- Call-in and online options for viewers
- Chat function
- Host dashboard
- Recording of webinar.

ADVANCED FEATURES:

- Customizable broadcast page
- Replay page
- Pre-recorded webinar plays as live
- Email automation and CRM lead management built in
- Handouts
- Polling and Q&A
- Reporting and Analytics.

5 EXAMPLE PLATFORMS:

- Basic: https://hangouts.google.com (Free; not full webinar functionality. Use the Hangouts On Air option to allow participants to view your broadcast with up to 10 people on air through video.)
- Basic: https://www.join.me
- Normal: http://www.anymeeting.com
- Advanced: https://www.gotomeeting.com
- Advanced: http://webinarjam.com (is an add-on that works with Google Hangouts)

3) COMMUNICATE WITH YOUR PARTICIPANTS AND PROSPECTS (EMAIL)

Leading up to the group, in between sessions, and as follow-up, you will need to communicate directly to your group members. Of course, the primary way to do this is via email.

Basic Email—It is possible to manually email your group members using a basic email system, such as Gmail, Yahoo or even Outlook. However, a more advanced email system that allows you to email the entire group as a whole would be a more efficient use of your time. Plus, if you try to send an email through one of those services to more than 10 people, it will often get marked as spam or end up in the receiver's junk mail bin.

Email Marketing Automation—Having a more robust email program is an added benefit for the *Marketing* aspect of running a coaching group. In the Creating a Marketing Campaign section, we discuss the details of what to include in your marketing campaigns. Some email programs have very advanced features that you may or may not need. Pricing depends on features and number of contacts, and some even offer free plans.

BASIC FEATURES:

- Customizable email templates
- Analytics that allow you to track who opens and clicks
- Basic Autoresponders (automatic emails that go up when a user registers and continue a pre-designed sequence by date)
- Email Series (a series of email autoresponders pre-timed to go out at certain times)

EXAMPLE PLATFORM:

- ConstantContact.com ($20–$100/month)

ADVANCED FEATURES:

- Marketing Automation Level 1: Responsive Campaigns (a series of email autoresponders that goes out based on the individual customer's behavior, interests, and previous sales)
- A/B Testing to try out headlines
- CRM (advanced contact management)

EXAMPLE PLATFORMS:

- ActiveCampaign.com ($9–$175/month)
- MailChimp.com (Free–$225/month)

BONUS FEATURES:

- Marketing Automation Level 2: Sales/Launch Funnels (pre-designed templates of responsive campaigns/series of autoresponders)
- Landing Pages (templates for opt-in pages and sales pages)
- Webinars
- Affiliate Programs
- Membership Programs
- Course/Content Delivery

EXAMPLE PLATFORMS:

- GetResponse.com: responsive campaigns, landing pages, webinars ($15–$165/month)

- WishPond.com: responsive campaigns, landing pages ($45–$129/month)

- ClickFunnels.com: responsive campaigns, sales funnels, landing pages, affiliate program, membership program ($97–$297/month)

- OptimizePress: No email (must use with a separate email program) landing pages, sales funnels, online courses (works with WordPress sites only) ($97–$297 one-time fee)

- Leadpages.net: advanced landing pages ONLY (can use with a separate email program) ($25–$80/month)

4) ENABLE PARTICIPANTS TO CONNECT WITH EACH OTHER

Having a virtual location where group members can communicate with each other *Outside* of the actual session is essential for any type of group. This feature gives participants an opportunity to share ideas, receive feedback, discuss the material, network with each other, or collaborate at a deeper level. It also gives you the opportunity to answer questions and provide feedback that you do not have time to do in the group sessions. There are several common ways to create this group conversation:

Facebook—Facebook is a great way to communicate with your group members, and for them with each other. Groups can be created for each coaching group you run. Groups can be made *Private* so that only people who you invite to your group can access the group, comment, or see who is in it. Benefits include the fact that it's a free service and that most of your participants are probably already on Facebook. Having the connections directly on Facebook is also an easy way for them to connect personally outside of the group, if they wish. There is also a functionality for individuals or small groups to have conversations through the Messenger functionality rather than inside the Facebook Group.

Find out more about setting up a Facebook group here: https://www.facebook.com/help/162866443847527/

Google Hangouts—Google Hangouts allows group members to

meet via video and talk to each other in groups up to 10. Great features include being able to easily switch the focus of the Hangout to the person who is currently talking. You can also share documents, YouTube videos, scratchpads, and images. As already mentioned, the Hangouts On Air option allows unlimited participants to view the video cast and up to 10 participants to join via video.

Find out more here: https://hangouts.google.com

5) CONTENT DELIVERY SYSTEM

If your program is structured and you are delivering training, informational or educational material, you will need a professional and user-friendly means of doing this.

Written—If your material is primarily written, you have several options:

- Email it directly to your clients
- Upload the files to your website and provide a link
- Upload through your webinar program, if it has that functionality
- For larger files, you can also use file sharing service such as Dropbox.com, Hightail.com, or others.

Video—There are a number of ways to deliver video instructions that your clients will watch prior to your group meetings. Some coaches teach all material live during sessions. Others have pre-recorded material which participants watch in between sessions. There are a number of options, based on your needs:

- **File Sharing**: You can use one of the file-sharing programs above. However, many of them have limits on file size and videos tend to be very large.
- **YouTube**: You can upload videos to YouTube for free and make them *Private*, meaning only people whom you send the link to can view them. You can either email links to your participants or embed the videos in your website.
- **Vimeo**: Vimeo works similar to YouTube. However, it has higher capacity, better privacy, and advanced features for implementing a full *course* into your website, such as through a WordPress plugin.

Online Course—If you have extensive content that you are delivering through video, outside of your *live* sessions, consider making it into a fully structured online course.

- **Video and WordPress:** You can build an online course directly on your website. This is a great way to do it if you already have a robust website, especially if you have a membership where participants already sign in. Specifically, there are pre-designed plug-ins that you can use with a WordPress site that will allow you to create a fully functional course. You can use YouTube or Vimeo videos with these plug-ins. Explore several options here: https://www.cminds.com/10-wordpress-plugins-e-learning/

- **Educational Platform:** Using a professional educational platform allows you to create a complete course, including video lectures, handout attachments, and even a built-in forum in many cases. They are easy to use for you (very low-tech) and provide very user-friendly and clean experience for your trainees. You can also easily track individual participant's progress.

An important feature to look for is the ability to *Drip Content.* This means programming the course to become available in sections, one week at a time or in time with your course outline. Participants will receive an email inviting them to the next section and the new material will become available when you schedule it to. One example of such an educational platform, that we recommend, is www.thinkific.com.

CHAPTER 3: GROUP FACILITATION SKILLS AND TIPS

LASER SPEAK

Laser speak is efficient, targeted speaking: It helps the speaker zero-in on the core of their ideas, concepts, information, and experiences and avoid storytelling or long explanations.

BENEFITS OF LASER SPEAK IN GROUPS:

- Creates an energetic exchange of ideas
- Maximizes group time together
- Keeps sessions on schedule
- Helps prevent one or more participants from dominating the group
- Gives all participants an opportunity to contribute
- Encourages participants to listen attentively because things move fast and they may miss something
- Helps participants sharpen their thinking and clarify their perspectives

GUIDELINES FOR LASER SPEAK:

- Get to the point
- Use the fewest words possible in the shortest time
- Share your name before you speak

- Focus on one issue at a time. Consult the group before changing the subject.

Modeling: As the coach, it's your role to model how to speak in an efficient, focused, targeted way. You also need to cover this in the first session to ensure the group understands the importance of being succinct and brief.

You will also need to gently remind the group, especially during the first few meetings, of the agreement to use laser speak. Reminders should be general rather than calling out individuals.

Use pre-session updates: Prior to each session, send a quick email with a basic outline of the session, the key outcomes or topics, and how participants should prepare. This saves time during the session and encourages laser focus.

LASER COACHING

As life coaches, laser coaching is used for quick alignment, a rapid way of relief, and a way of quickly unblocking someone who may have felt stuck in their way of thinking for a long time. Coaches use laser coaching to address a single issue, concern, opportunity or challenge. Usually, laser sessions are conducted in a short period of time (often around 15 minutes). Laser sessions can be longer when focused on a more complex issue. However, the focus is on being specific, prepared and succinct.

LASER COACHING AN INDIVIDUAL IN THE GROUP

One way to integrate laser coaching in your group program is to coach an individual group member *live* while conducting the group session. Having a group member in the "hot seat" provides an opportunity to help an individual overcome a pressing challenge while instantaneously guiding the other participants to their own answers. Everyone benefits from the teachable moment of a *live* laser coaching session.

INCLUDING LASER COACHING IN YOUR PROGRAM

Laser sessions are extremely beneficial when you're working with a group that is working on individual goals. Since each participant doesn't get a chance to discuss his or her personal situation in the group discussion, providing laser sessions can help individuals move forward, gain clarity, or make decisions. After a laser session, participants may be more focused and able to benefit from the group.

Consider setting aside a few hours to schedule laser sessions for your group members who are interested. You can set appointments for 10–15 minute sessions (4 per hour). Set the expectation that callers must be prepared to jump right to the point, having clarified what they want to accomplish. You'd be amazed at how much you can accomplish in such a short time when you're focused!

GROUP LASER COACHING

Another way to use laser coaching in your group is to laser coach *as* a group. Often, this works like a laser round table in which the entire group provides feedback to one individual.

- Conduct a round table discussion in which one participant shares a specific question or challenge they have, and then each person in the group shares a key point, question, or wisdom about the scenario (ideally 30 seconds each, longer in very small groups).

- About 10 minutes is enough time to brainstorm the scenario, after which time ask the participant who shared his or her concern with the group to identify two takeaways from the group discussion. Then move on. If time allows and there is a specific outcome you are trying to accomplish from the group laser session, it's okay to extend the time.

- Then, ask the group to reflect on how that individual's experience and the ideas generated in the group could be valuable to everyone else in the group. This helps all participants apply the learning points to their own lives.

2 TIPS FOR LASER COACHING IN GROUPS

Ask the client to identify a specific concern, problem, opportunity or block they wish to address ahead of time.

Whether coaching the individual *live* or privately, ask them to share their concern (succinctly) through email with you ahead of time (so you can prepare and save time).

ROLE-PLAYING

Role-playing has many benefits and it is something that, if used properly, can truly reinforce behaviors, patterns, and tools that clients are working on in the group. We have used role-playing in many groups, workshops, and training and have found it to be a great tool. The other benefits of role-playing include:

- **Helps build confidence:** By utilizing role-playing, you can create a safe environment to practice different scenarios that group members may face in the real word or try out new skills. This practice builds confidence in things that will help them in their day-to-day roles.

- **Helps develop listening skills:** Role-playing requires listening skills. The people in the role-play have to not only pay attention to the words being used but, when in person, also the nonverbal communication that provides valuable information. It is better to develop these communication skills in a safe place where they can get feedback with minimal resistance.

- **It allows space for creative problem-solving:** Creativity in solving challenges in life often comes from exposure and having past experience that you can draw upon when a new situation arises. Therefore, role-playing will at least give your group members an opportunity to develop some experience in handling difficult situations and in turn, develop their creative problem-solving skills.

There are two ways you can use role-playing. First, you can have two (or more) people act out a scenario with the rest of the group observing. Second, you can split the group into role-playing groups of 2 (or more) people and have *each* sub-group act out the role-play.

HOW TO USE ROLE-PLAY

It's easy to set up and run a role-playing session. Simply follow the five steps below.

Step 1: Identify the Situation: The first thing you need to do to start the process is gather people together. Then, introduce the problem or topic. Next, encourage an open discussion to get the different perspectives on the relevant issues within the topic. Having the discussion allows participants to start assessing and thinking about the problem before you begin the role-play. This allows people to become more comfortable with the topic. If the group is unfamiliar with each other, we suggest you start with an activity that will help them become more comfortable with each other.

Step 2: Add Details: After making sure that everyone is familiar with the problems, set up a scenario with enough detail so that it can feel like a real situation. Make sure that everyone understands the purpose of the role-play and what you are trying to achieve with it.

Step 3: Set Ground Rules: It's important to set ground rules so that the environment is supportive and the objective of the role-playing can be achieved. The people who are observing the role-play should also consider what feedback they can provide at the end of the role-play. One important ground rule should be that the role-play participants have the opportunity to call time out if they feel overwhelmed or want to take a break from their role. Also, make sure to frame the exercise as an opportunity to experiment with new skills and techniques that will help them in the real world. However, they are not expected to be perfect. Also, make sure that role-playing is brief—less than 5 minutes—to allow time to process the information.

Step 4: Assign Roles: Once you've developed a good foundation of the problem and set the scene, identify what roles each participant will have in the role-play. Also, specify who is role-playing—whether it's only one set of people, for demonstration, or if the entire group will split into small groups or pairs and role-play. Then, determine the roles. For example, one person may be the one bringing up the problem while another will be the one listening and addressing the other person's concerns. In other words, one person will play the role of the person dealing with the situation and another plays the role of the person who is either being supportive (like a coach) or hostile (like a client, loved one, co-worker, etc.) depending on the scenario.

Step 5: Do a Demonstration: Some people will have resistance to role-playing. Therefore, it may be important to make the experience less threatening by doing a demonstration before actually starting. You can have two participants who are the most outgoing or you can use one participant and yourself. You can also hand out prepared scripts and give the participants a few minutes to prepare. Then, you can have them act out the role-play in front of the rest of the group.

Step 6: Act Out the Scenario: First, arrange chairs for role-play participants (if applicable). At this point, each person will assume their roles and act out the situation. It may be easier to build on the intensity of the role-play as people get more comfortable with the role. You can also have participants try a new situation after a couple of minutes.

Step 7: Discuss What You Have Learned: When the role-play is finished, give the participants a couple of minutes to share feedback, and discuss what they have learned from the experience.

Step 8: Switch Roles: If participants are broken into subgroups, consider having participants switch roles so that everyone has the opportunity to play both roles. When the role-play is finished give the participants a couple of minutes to share feedback, and discuss what they have learned from the experience.

Step 9: Debriefing: In this step, you should have everyone have a discussion about the activity. Make sure to give positive feedback and reinforce what the purpose was of the activity. The group can share insights that they have learned, some of the challenges, and give feedback on how they can apply it to their life.

AVOIDING COMMON PROBLEMS

Fielding Difficult Questions: If you're asked a question you don't know how to answer or handle, throw it out to the Group to answer it—which may lead to a great answer and gives you time to come up with an answer or a clarifying question. If you genuinely do not know the answer, it's better to be honest than to fake it. Acknowledge that you don't have a good answer for them but you'll get back to them about it. Then, research or call someone who may be able to provide insight. And revisit the topic later, as promised, either in the group or personally.

Conflict within the Group: Most group coaches we've met say they rarely have problems with group members having conflict. This is because they do a good job establishing trust and an environment of respect and championing. But, even in this case, it's possible that there may be times when you sense tension in the group, which can be due to misunderstanding or disagreements. It is important to address this *immediately*—as soon as you notice it.

Direct your question in general, without calling anyone out. Express that you're feeling like there may be some frustration or tension. And ask if anyone has any insight as to what may be going on. Let the group know that your goal is to make sure everyone feels heard and can focus on the tasks at hand. Usually, the issue can be quickly addressed. If in any case someone is emotionally charged, behaves inappropriately or expresses they do not wish to discuss it publicly, address the situation after the session with the individual(s) involved.

Different Agendas: What if the group I'm working with is co-creating an agenda and cannot agree? As a coach, your job is to mediate in a situation like this. Be objective and suggest ways of organizing the agenda to include all ideas, or rearrange the agenda to address one area that day and another in the next session. In open coaching, each individual has their own personal agenda as well. There may be times a group can be split into subgroups if some members are interested in going one direction while others are not.

Commitment: So, what do you do if certain group members continuously fail to keep their commitments? Sharing commitments publicly often helps individuals stay more on track, as they do not want to have to face the group when they haven't followed through. While discussing progress in the group, ask individuals who haven't followed through to reflect on why they believe that is and re-commit from this greater place of clarity. If it happens repeatedly, it may be an indication that a laser session may be helpful. Ultimately, however, there are some people who simply will not follow through.

This can also apply to group members not showing up to sessions. Often, groups that are highly engaged will inquire with the missing party and encourage participation, since it affects everyone. When working in a group with a high level of collaboration, missing sessions may warrant you reaching out to them to determine what is preventing them from attending. However, in many groups, attendance will often not be at 100 percent. Usually, the more people pay for a program the more they attend.

Live Coaching: Often, we've heard group coaches express that they don't feel comfortable coaching an individual *live* in front of a group. First, you do not *have* to. In fact, many, if not most coaching groups, do not include *live* coaching. Second, you can have the entire group coach an individual with a laser round table (see the Session Structure section). Third, if you are afraid of having a topic come up that is too difficult to discuss in a short laser session in front of the group, there are two ways to tackle this:

- Pre-screen potential laser coaching clients by having them email you their question or concern ahead of time, and select the one you're comfortable with and you know can be succinct.

- In the event you're presented with a challenge you're not able to answer easily or would be too time consuming, simply state that the person's question would be more time-consuming than you have time for during the group session, and that you can follow up with them later, one-on-one. Then, ask the group if there is anyone who has a topic that could be addressed quickly.

Price Discrepancies: In many cases, the members of your group may have paid a different price to participate than other members in the group. Often, coaches are concerned that participants will find out that they paid a different price than someone else. One way to deal with this is to be upfront about your price differentiation. Let the group know (possibly in the agreement) that a few scholarships may be awarded for specific reasons, some participants receive their entry as part of a package, and/or discounts are given for participants who refer other clients (or whatever the case may be). Now, in truth, there may be free or discounted participants for other reasons. However, addressing that there will be some price differentiation will avoid the question and if it does come up, you can refer back to the disclosure.

DEALING WITH CHALLENGING PARTICIPANTS

If you do enough groups, you will soon realize that there will be on occasion difficult group members and that issues will emerge. This is especially true when people do not feel valued or heard. This is why it is critical to spend time building trust among the group members and spending time getting to know them so you can know their needs and personality characteristics and how to deal with them. However, keep in mind that having a difficult participant is not a reflection of you. It's a natural phenomenon that can be seen in many groups regardless of topic or structure.

Tip: To better know your participants before the group starts, one option is to have them complete a simple survey that helps you get to know them. And the other is to schedule a one-on-one 15-minute call with each participant. This will allow you to become more familiarized with them, what brought them to the program, and what they want to get out of it.

POINTS TO BEAR IN MIND AS YOU DEAL WITH DIFFICULT PARTICIPANTS:

Your clients bring with them their own perspective in life and unique experiences that filter how they perceive their reality.

- Your clients have a natural creativity, are resourceful and are whole. As a coach, you serve as a facilitator to help your clients utilize what they have to help them transform.
- Your clients have the foundation they need and are capable of making their own life decisions whether you agree with them or not. As a coach, your role is to help them connect with their own insights, wisdom, and empower them to help make their own decisions.
- It is your role to help your clients understand their roles as well as your own role in the process.

10 TYPES OF DIFFICULT PARTICIPANTS AND WHAT TO DO WITH THEM:

1. The Shy or Quiet One
2. The Challenger
3. The Dominator
4. The Unfocused
5. The Super Achiever
6. The Center of Attention
7. The Joker
8. The Devil's Advocate
9. The Argumentative One
10. The Sidebar

We will assess each one of these participants and give you tips on how to deal with them.

1. The Shy or Quiet One: It is important to remember that we have different personalities and temperaments. Some participants will naturally be shy and feel uncomfortable in a group. Therefore, do not assume that someone being shy is due to lack of interest or engagement in the process. Therefore, include a variety of ways that people can communicate or participate in the process so that they can engage, reflect, and learn.

If someone is extremely shy, they may benefit from a smaller more intimate group. They may also benefit from small group or partnership activities within the group where they are not forced to be put on the spot in front of the whole group. Include them in a way that they feel safe to participate. In some types of group coaching that don't have a high level of engagement, this is not relevant. However, if the interaction of the group is valuable to a highly engaged group, one way to encourage participation of a quiet individual is to bring up topics you know they have something of value to contribute.

If you have members complete an intake questionnaire that helps you learn about why they're joining the group, what their interests and concerns are, and what value they have to offer the group, you can refer to this questionnaire to determine what you may be able to use as bait for discussion with this individual.

2. The Challenger: This participant can present many obstacles for the coach and other participants. This participant will want to challenge what you say and what other people in the group share. As a coach, it is important to continually reinforce the fact that we all have different life experiences, desires, perceptions, and ways of dealing with things, and that they can choose to take away from what is being shared only the things that resonate and feel right to them. Therefore, they are the expert about their own journey and that everyone's role in a group is to respect each other's view and life experiences and share tools, insights, and a different perspective to help each other grow in their own, unique ways.

3. The Dominator: You will typically have one person in the group who wants to dominate the group. The person may steal the show, talk over others, and/or go off on tangents. Sometimes, a person simply doesn't know when to stop talking. The first response is to use a coaching skill called intruding, in which you interject or jump-in in the middle of their statement to either ask a probing question or highlight an area that they shared that's relevant. This stops the freight train. Also, it is important to remind the group about laser speak regularly—not when the person is already talking. Reminders should be general rather than calling out individuals. Praising when someone does a good job at laser speak reinforces the importance of it.

4. The Unfocused One: This participant can seem to wander off often and not be fully engaged. You need to remember that how each person processes information can affect their focus. One of the best things to do is to let the group know what you will be going over, the importance of each item, and how it applies to their life. If a person's mind can answer *why* they should stay focused, they will do a better job at staying with you.

Also, make sure the participants know what they want and their purpose for being in the group. The clearer a person is about their purpose, the more invested they will be. In a non-engaged group, this is ultimately their choice. In a fully engaged group, in which their lack of focus affects the whole group, you may need to discuss it with them. If they continue to be unfocused and uninterested, you may have to ask yourself if the client is coachable, and if they are truly ready to make a commitment to the process.

5. The Super Achiever: Having someone who is a super achiever may sound great. However, it can pose a challenge for the coach and the group as it may make other group members feel inadequate, like there is something wrong with them, leading to de-motivation. Therefore, it is important to reinforce the fact that everyone will be moving at their own pace within the group, and that it is okay. It is important to also let the participants know that achievements, success, and wins are defined differently for everyone, and that it is important to celebrate both small and large achievements. Having the super achiever express what they have learned from their experience may help give the other participants insights, and at the same time, serve as inspiration.

6. The Center of Attention: You may also find someone in the group who likes to be the center of attention. We have found that giving the person a role or responsibility helps them meet their need for the spotlight, and at the same time, helps meet the group's needs. For example, the person can be the note taker, the person who writes on the board, the time keeper, and so on. This is also a great area to explore with the person in a one-on-one session as it can help them understand why they have this need and how it impacts them and others. For example, you can ask questions such as: *"What's important about being seen?"*, *"What happens when you are not seen?"*, and *"What impact does it have on others?"*

7. The Joker: Having someone who brings humor to the group is very beneficial to the coaching process. However, if it is constant or extreme, it can also take away from the importance of some topics and impact the group in a negative way. One thing you can do is to have the group discuss in what ways humor can add value to the group, such as during certain topics. They can also discuss when group members feel it would not be appreciated.

Many times, the joker has not reflected on the impact of the group. The group discussion may help but another alternative is to have a private conversation in which you share with them the value of what they bring to the group, and then have them reflect on the fact that there may be topics or times that using humor may negatively impact communication. Empower him or her to determine ways you could work as a team to help the group utilize his or her skills at the appropriate times.

8. The Devil's Advocate: The Devil's Advocate can bring a lot of value to the group, as they bring a different perspective that the group or an individual has not considered. It also serves as a great reminder that there may be many ways to view any situation. It is important to reinforce the value of this in the group and to remind everyone that we all may have a different perspective. And, that it's not about being right or wrong but finding the perspective that will help us live in integrity with ourselves and what we want to create.

9. The Argumentative One: Some individuals will want to argue for argument's sake. It may be easy to either answer with a reflective question such as, "What is at stake?" or "What do you hope to gain from your complaint?" so that they can reflect whether there is a point to the argument. On the other hand, many times, it is easier to defer the situation to the group. For example, you can ask what others in the group think. Do they agree with the issue being raised or item being challenged? Do they feel that it needs further discussion? If no one feels like it is important, then you can have the group move on and let the participant know that you would be more than willing to address it with them after the group session ends. Many times, they would have forgotten why they wanted to argue in the first place by the time the group session ends.

10. The Sidebar: This is more typical in larger groups, in-person groups, and especially after coming back from a group activity, break, or transition. This is when two or more participants are having a conversation while you or another participant is trying to speak.

Many times, an open invitation to share with the group or glancing over to them will be enough to help the participants to either become part of the group discussion or stop their conversation. However, when that does not work, you can move toward where the conversation is happening (if you are walking around). Or, you can remind the group that you want to make sure everyone is respecting others when they are talking by giving their full attention, and end it with a statement such as "Thank you everyone for understanding." If you are using technology that allows it, you can "mute" their lines. Then, casually go back to what was being discussed. Many times, if you do it in a non-confrontational, casual manner, people will respect the boundaries. If it becomes a problem, then make sure to address it with the members individually after the group session ends.

GROUP CLOSURE (LASER TAKEAWAYS)

During a group coaching session, there may be different emotions that come up, both positive and negative. There could be moments of insight or moments of processing information that can be transformational to a participant's life. Therefore, it is important to make sure that you end each session with an activity that will help people leave in a good state and with an idea of what they will be working on moving forward. This closure process helps them fully integrate the experience. In all of the following examples, it's important to use laser-speak to keep the activity short. We also refer to these as *laser takeaways*.

Closure Circle: Have each participant share with the group one insight that they have learned and how they will be applying it and integrating it into their life. This will help members reinforce to each other what they have learned. If in person, sit participants in a circle.

Appreciations: Have the group members share something that they appreciated about the group: a member in the group or something from session. This activity, if done consistently, will help the participants unconsciously look for things to be grateful for in future sessions.

Action Plan: One important activity is for the group members to share with the group their next step, goal, and what they are committing to before the next meeting. They can also state who they will be accountable to. Since you do not want them to forget, make sure that they write it down since it will reinforce their commitment. If it is a large group, you can have them split into smaller groups or partnerships to share their goals or even share answers to two or three structured questions.

Nature Walk and Closure: For in person groups, to add a creative twist, you can allow participants 5 to 10 minutes to do a silent walk in the surrounding environment (if venue permits), and have them select a piece of nature which they bring back into the program (i.e., stone/flower/leaf). Participants can then close with a discussion of what they have chosen and also what they are taking away from the group session, which they'll share in the closure circle format. A neat thing about it is that participants can take this object home with them as a reminder of their learning and commitments.

Laughter Session: This is one of the favorite activities that we undertake to close out sessions and to change participants' state to one of happiness and joy before our clients leave. You can look up group laughter activates on YouTube to get some ideas. We also have a full course on this topic, if you are interested in learning more about implementing it in your practice.

Sample Questions You Can Use:

- What is one thing you learned today and how will you apply it to your life?
- What are you grateful for today when it comes to the group, a member, or the session?
- What is your next step and goal that you are committing to before the next meeting?

CHAPTER 4: COMMUNICATION TECHNIQUES

CHAMPIONING THE GROUP

Championing involves celebrating and encouraging who our clients are and what they want. It means recognizing and praising them for their accomplishments and contributions to the group. One notable distinction is to recognize the difference between championing and cheerleading. Cheerleading is an emotional reaction or comment that, while may convey excitement, is usually general and does not necessarily identify a specific accomplishment. Cheerleading may sound encouraging, but it can be too easy to say something that may not come across as genuine. Championing, however, provides feedback on a group member's specific success, strength or action. The key to championing is *celebration* and *feedback*.

KEYS TO CHAMPIONING IN A GROUP:

- Encourage participants to celebrate other group members' successes.
- Highlight an individual's success and remind each member to celebrate themselves.
- Base your championing on truth (don't say something encouraging just to say it).
- Give positive feedback in the moment it happens. "Did everyone hear what David just said? Wasn't that a great point?"
- Give positive feedback in terms of your personal opinion or feelings, not as a judgment or critique. "It was powerful how you

took responsibility for your mistake and apologized immediately." (opinion) vs. "You handled that situation well." (judgment).

- Do not over-praise the group or individuals. Avoid inflated language, such as "fantastic" or "incredible."
- Be specific about what you are encouraging.
- Praise, celebrate and provide positive feedback regularly.

USE "WHEN, WHAT, HOW" STATEMENTS

Being specific will make the person feel like you are not judging their whole character, but rather looking at a specific behavior. Instead of generalizing with always or never, get specific. This can be for a positive statement or a negative one.

BELOW ARE ADDITIONAL COMMUNICATION TIPS FOR COACHING GROUPS:

- Use "I" statements.
- Ask clarifying questions, not leading ones.
- Identify opportunities for specific member input. If there is a participant with experience or expertise that others can benefit from, call on them for input when something comes up which you know they could add value to.
- Listen for coaching opportunities rather than just passively listening as they speak or interact.
- Listen without making any assumptions and ask for clarity if necessary.

ACTIVE LISTENING

The purpose of listening is to obtain information, learn about the other's perspective, gain deeper understanding, and enjoy the process.

As a coach, you should be doing:

70% listening

30% questioning

When coaching:

- Give your client your full attention
- Look at them
- No distractions: Do not have anything around you to distract you (don't be on your computer or phone, doing anything else, have others around, etc.)
- Take notes

4 STEPS TO EFFECTIVE, ACTIVE LISTENING:

Step 1: Listen

Step 2: Acknowledge

Step 3: Clarify *(reflective listening or paraphrasing)*

Step 4: Respond

1. Start at 1 again
2. Discuss options
3. Ask a question

REFLECTIVE LISTENING

PARAPHRASING WHILE COACHING

Paraphrasing is repeating, in your words, what you interpreted someone else to be saying. Paraphrasing helps your client know you are fully paying attention. Even more importantly, paraphrasing helps you make sure you understood what they said correctly, leading to further clarity.

Essential tips for paraphrasing:

- Put the focus of the paraphrase on what the other person implied, not on what you wanted him/her to imply; e.g., don't say, "I believe what you meant to say was …" Instead, say "If I'm hearing you right, you conveyed that …?"
- Phrase the paraphrase as a question, "So you're saying that …?" so that the other person has the responsibility and opportunity to refine his/her original comments in response to your question.
- Put the focus of the paraphrase on the other person; e.g., if the

person said, "I don't get enough resources to do what I want," then don't paraphrase, "We probably all don't get what we want, right?"

- Put the ownership of the paraphrase on yourself; e.g., "If I'm hearing you right …?" or "If I understand you correctly …?"

- Put the ownership of the other person's words on him/her; e.g., say "If I understand you right, you're saying that …?" or "… you believe that …?" or "… you feel that …?"

- In the paraphrase, use some of the words that the other person used. For example, if the other person said, "I think we should do more planning around here," you might paraphrase, "If I'm hearing you right in this strategic planning workshop, you believe that more strategic planning should be done in our community?"

- Don't judge or evaluate the other person's comments; e.g., don't say, "I wonder if you really believe that?" or "Don't you feel out-on-a-limb making that comment?"

- You can use a paraphrase to validate your impression of the other person's comments; e.g., you could say, "So you were frustrated when …?"

- The paraphrase should be shorter than the original comments made by the other person.

- If the other person responds to your paraphrase that you still don't understand him/her, then give the other person 1–2 chances to restate his position. Then you might cease the paraphrasing; otherwise, you might embarrass or provoke the other person.

EMPATHETIC LISTENING

Empathetic listening is paying attention to another person with empathy (identifying their emotional state). Active listening and paraphrasing is when you repeat back to the person what you think she or he said to make certain you understand. Empathetic listening is when you ask how the person feels about the situation or make a statement about how you believe the person feels. Empathetic listening goes beyond simply acknowledging what the client is saying. In empathetic listening, you acknowledge how the client is feeling, even if they aren't saying it.

For example, a student might say, "My dog got hit by a car this morning." An active listening response might be, "Your dog got hit by a car?"

or "Was it hurt?" An empathetic response might be, "I can see this has upset you. Do you want to talk about it?"

SYMPATHY VS. EMPATHY

Empathy is not sympathy. Whereas sympathy is *feeling for some-one*, empathy is *feeling as someone*. For example, you may feel badly for your client, or better put—feeling about their situation. To differentiate, many people say that empathy is *putting yourself in their shoes* and feel-ing as they would.

Listening empathetically means being able to put *yourself* aside. It requires listening without judgment, even when you have an opposing view or disagree with your client. It differentiates between acknowledg-ing and approving or agreeing. Your opinion is irrelevant. You aren't try-ing to solve their problem. You are simply listening, fully, and tuning into how they are feeling.

Putting yourself aside also means refraining from imagining how *You* would feel if it were *You*. Sound contradictory? It's not. And here is where many people go wrong with their understanding of empathy and putting themselves in other people's shoes.

First, let's discuss another commonly misunderstood concept.

The Golden Rule: Do unto others the way you would have them do unto you.

Most people interpret this as: determine how you would want others to treat you and then treat them that way. This point seems simple enough if you're talking about respect or being polite. But the simple example of someone being sick quickly shows the error in this interpretation of the golden rule. When you are sick, do you enjoy being doted on and having someone take care of you? Or, do you prefer to be left alone in peace? If you prefer the doting, you may—while trying to use the golden rule—dote on others who are sick. But what if they prefer to be left alone? You are doing unto them as *You* would want done unto you. But, it's not what *they* want. They want to be left alone. And so here is the true meaning of the golden rule:

Determine what others would want done unto them and do that. That is what you would want done for you, isn't it?

73

Now, let's look at *empathy is putting yourself in another person's shoes*. Where many people get hung up is that they imagine themselves being in the same position as the other person, asking themselves "How would I feel if it were me?" However, when they do this, they are putting *themselves* into the situation. It's good—it's closer to empathy, but if they look down, they'll see they are wearing their *own* shoes, not the shoes of the other person.

> *Therefore, to truly empathize, you must take on your client's perspective, not your own.*

Rather than viewing what your client is expressing (saying or feeling) through your own filters—your own experiences, your own beliefs, your own feelings—your goal is to remain open and be able to understand them from their own perspective.

- Am I feeling bad for my client? If so, it's sympathy.

- Am I talking too much or relating their situation to something in my own life experience? If so, it's not a bad thing. But it would be better if you noticed this, and shifted your attention back to your client. Resist any temptation to talk about yourself in order to find common ground. First, just listen and focus on *your client*, not you.

- Am I imagining myself being in their position? If so, good… now take it one step further and check if you still have your shoes on. Remove all judgmental thoughts, such as "this is bad." Instead of thinking "If this were *me*, I would feel ___" ask yourself, "If I were *them*, knowing what I know about them, I how would I feel?" If you don't know enough about them and their situation to differentiate between how they may be feeling vs. how they would feel, ask additional questions.

The point here is that just because you feel emotional regarding what your client is expressing does not necessarily mean you are empathizing. It is important to know that you are feeling your *own* emotions, not theirs, and to practice minimizing this. To pick up on someone else's emotion, first you must stop having your own. Then, you can pick up another's feelings empathetically by observing cues of their physical state—tears, tone of voice, posture, language, expression, etc. and even feeling their energetic field. You can then take their perspective, as if you were *them* and imagine what it would be like. In this case, your empathy is based on observation and carefully assuming their position rather than your knee jerk emotional response.

The goal of empathetic listening is to listen and respond to your client in a way that:

a) Increases your true understanding of their perspective, frame of reference, and feelings.

b) Makes them feel understood, affirmed, validated and that they can trust you.

By doing this, you can more accurately perceive your client's true desires and guide them appropriately. By showing your client you are listening and understanding them, you develop trust and respect and it promotes them being more likely to hear you when you need to coach them to push through their resistance or obstacles.

For example, in a hospital, a nurse might say after listening to a patient: *"I hear that you are very uncomfortable right now, Susan, and you would really like to get out of that bed and move around. But your doctor says your bones won't heal unless you stay put for another week."* The patient in this example is much more likely to listen to the nurse if the nurse simply said: *"I'm really sorry, Susan, but you have to stay in bed. Your doctor says your bones won't heal unless you stay put for another week."* What is missing in this second version is any acknowledgment of the patient's present experience.

STEPS TO EMPATHETIC LISTENING:

4. Provide the speaker with your undivided attention.

5. Be non-judgmental. Don't minimize or trivialize the speaker's issue. Don't confuse it with your own issue.

6. Read the speaker's state. Observe the emotions behind the words. Is the speaker angry, afraid, frustrated, resistant, or resentful? Respond to the emotion as well as the words.

7. Be quiet. Don't feel you must have an immediate reply. Often, if you allow for some quiet time after the client has expressed themselves, they themselves will break the silence and offer a solution.

8. Assure your understanding. Ask clarifying questions and restate what you perceive the speaker to be saying *and*, specifically, feeling.

The last step then is to move forward with the coaching process of giving them your observations, feedback, and examples and then discussing options and strategies for change.

CHAPTER 5: MARKETING AND FILLING YOUR GROUPS

IDENTIFYING YOUR MARKET

Most coaches love coaching and hate marketing. Welcome to the club!

But, marketing doesn't have to be a mystery or miserable. Targeting your marketing is the first key to having marketing that is more effective and more enjoyable. Using proven strategies is the second key, and we'll get to that later.

Targeting your market requires doing a little **market research**.

STEP 1: WHO IS YOUR MARKET?

- Who are your ideal clients, specifically for this group?
- What are they passionate about?
- What struggles do they have which you can provide solutions for?
- Are they already familiar with coaching and/or group programs?

STEP 2: WHERE CAN I REACH THEM?

- Do you already have contact with a large number of people in your market, such as an email list?
- Do you have individual clients who may be interested in your group?
- Do you have an engaged social network who you could get excited about an upcoming group by offering a free teleseminar or webinar or even sharing an article or tips related to your group

content? (See the section *Creating a Marketing Campaign*.)

- Do you have colleagues, joint venture partners, or other collaborators whom you could collaborate on a group with or whom you could present an introductory presentation or workshop to?

- Are there organizations you're familiar with or know of that work with your population and whom may be interested in having you present to or form a group for their staff?

- Can you think of anyone else you know who has direct access to these people? (Who?)

- Where else could you find these people, online or in person? (Think about what their interests are.)

- Who is the *easiest* to find or connect to and where are they?

STEP 3: WHAT DO THEY WANT?

*See the sample **This is For You** promotion on the next page that shows how you can use this information to reflect back to your prospects that you "get them" and help them know if your program is for them.*

- If you feel this market would be interested in your group, *why* would they be interested—from *their* perspective?

- What pain do they have that is worth the investment to take away the pain?

- What outcomes would they be looking for?

- How do you believe they would want the program structured, that would be convenient, motivational and useful for them? If you're not sure about what they want—especially what they want a group program to be like—consider *asking them*! You could conduct a survey, a focus group, or ask current clients.

Marketing Example: The *This is For You* List: (next page)

Are you ready to soar?

You are an ideal candidate for the *Women Who Soar* group coaching program if:

- You feel overwhelmed and exhausted by all the demands on you professionally and personally—you want more peace and balance.

- It seems like there just isn't enough time to get everything done —you need to calm the chaos and take back control of your time.

- You are unsure what action to take and feel confused—you want to awaken your intuition and feel more confident about your decisions.

- You are ready to take responsibility for your life and stop blaming other people or external circumstances—you are ready to make empowered choices.

- The stress you are under is making work less joyful or affecting your health and your personal relationships—you want to stress less and thrive more.

You are not alone! Many of us feel this way but don't do anything about it. Somehow, it becomes the new normal and you begin to believe that everything won't get done.

You may also talk yourself out of asking for what you want because you don't want to create conflict or upset anyone. You resign yourself to believing that stress is part of life, work isn't supposed to be joyful, and you just have to deal with it.

If any of this resonates with you, you are in the right place. I am here to help you. You need tools and techniques, support and encouragement, and a solid action plan to move you forward.

I have pulled together all of the best information I've shared with hundreds of clients over the years, proven tools and techniques, and the power of coaching and group synergy. I am offering it to you at a discounted package price. There are limited spots available. So, if this feels right for you, please reserve your spot today.

Come soar with us! You are ready for this.

Note: Make sure you target different segments of your market differently. For example, if you're a career coach, there is a very different process for marketing to and coaching a college student vs. a mid-life career changer vs. a retiree. Each may be interested in career coaching. However, the marketing strategy and group coaching program for each would be very different.

If you don't yet feel like you've clearly identified your ideal target market—your tribe—and you want to make sure you're narrowed in on an ideal niche, check out our course TARGET MARKETING: Identify Your Tribe and Niche *course. And, if you feel your marketing copy could use an upgrade, consider our course* Write Epic Marketing and Sales Copy. *Find out more at the end of the book.*

CREATING A MARKETING CAMPAIGN

Instead of stressing about marketing or randomly shooting in the dark, create a campaign designed to fill your group and then use it over and over again.

Important requirements of a successful marketing campaign:

- Builds excitement/momentum
- Coordinates sequences of activities
- Delivers huge value and inspires action
- Education-based marketing… focuses on providing value
- Demonstrates your expertise
- Makes an emotional connection with your audience
- Positions your group (offering a solution they need)

Possible elements of your marketing campaign:

- Emails
- Advertising (such as Facebook)
- Website
- Teleseminars/Webinars

- Google hangout
- Livestream
- Speaking
- Workshops
- Videos

The Magic Trifecta: We're going to focus on **emails**, key **website** elements, and **webinars** (with calls-to-action) because this trifecta has been proven to be the most effective process for enrolling clients into group coaching programs.

We will *not* go over the process for creating a webinar in this program. However, there are many resources available to teach you how to run a webinar. *We also have a course called* Get Life Coaching Clients with Workshops *that helps you design a presentation (which can be used in a webinar) that provides tremendous value, teaches valuable information, and also entices attendees to register for your program (IN A WAY THAT DOES NOT FEEL OR SOUND "SALESY!) Find out more at the end of the book.*

Teleseminars, Google Hangouts and livestreams are alternatives to the webinar. Speaking and workshops are great first-level contacts with potential clients and can be used as a way to market your group or sign people up to attend a webinar, that then signs them up for your group.

Videos can be used in your email campaigns to add value.

Advertising, including on Facebook, is beyond the scope of this course. However, there are many trainings out there.

SIMPLE MARKETING CAMPAIGN EXAMPLE:

- In-person luncheon workshop (promoted through Facebook and networking events). At the end, an irresistible offer is made to participants to join your group.
- Webinar (repurposes the material from the presentation) or alternatively allow access to a livestream of the *live* event or a replay of a recording from the event (also both marketed through Facebook or in person). At the end, an irresistible offer is made to participants to join your group.
- Email autoresponder campaign to follow up with **a)** people who

expressed interest but didn't sign up for the *live* event (telling them about the livestream or recorded alternatives), **b)** people who signed up for the *live* event but didn't come (to remind them of the online recording), and **c)** people who attended either the in-person or online component (providing value and offering participation in the group or other products and services).

Once this campaign is established, it can be used over and over...

KEY WEBSITE ELEMENTS AND HOW TO USE THEM TO MARKET YOUR GROUPS

Sales Pages:

While many people put a great deal of time and effort into building a website, they often miss this one simple page that sells more products than any well-made website: *The Sales Page*. A website contains a lot of information and is often difficult to navigate. Add to that how most people don't have good *calls to action* (more on that later), and it's no wonder so many coaches get very little business from their websites.

On the other hand, a well-made Sales Page focuses exclusively on a particular program or product and eliminates distractions, which keeps visitors' attention directed where you want it. It also speaks directly to the visitor, answers their questions, and entices them to sign up for whatever you're offering.

We've included a <u>Sales Page Template</u> *and some industry best practices and tips to get you started building a sales page for your group!*

Once you have your sales page, next you need to get traffic to it! There are two ways to do this:

- The 1-Step Familiarity Method
- The 2-Step Prospecting Method

The 1-Step Familiarity Method capitalizes on the clients, prospects, and contacts you already have. This can include your email list, current clients, or even people you meet at networking events or pick up a flyer of yours at an event that's related to what you do. In each case, these people already know, like and trust you to one degree or another. You can reach out to them through email or in person and direct them to your sales page. One downside is that you don't know who actually *goes* to your sales page—you only know who they are if the sign up. This means there is no way to follow up with interested parties.

The 2-Step Prospecting Model uses an Opt-In Page that offers an entry-level product, such as an informational webinar, which then leads interested parties to your Sales Page.

Opt-In Page:

Also referred to as a **Landing Page**, an Opt-In Page is designed to help you get new prospects, rather than directly sell visitors on your group program. The Opt-In-Page is **step 1** and to promote your group program, it is recommended to have this page offer a high-value free training (i.e., webinar, teleseminar, free video training, etc.). The *key* here, to get visitors to **step 2**—your Sales Page—is to make sure that at the end of your webinar/teleseminar/video, you invite them to join the group. For example, "If you liked this webinar and would like to learn how to implement _____, I have a group program that offers_____." Explain the benefits, the program, and how to find out more by visiting the link to your Sales Page.

The great thing about Opt-In Pages is that once your prospects opt-in, **you have their contact information** and know who they are! This means that even if they **a)** don't follow through on attending the webinar or **b)** attend the webinar and do not register for your group, you can still contact them to either remind them of the group or offer a different product or service (using an email autoresponder—see below).

Determine your giveaway. This is your freebie, the irresistible tasty nugget of wisdom you want to share to inspire site visitors to sign up, give you their email address, and have the opportunity to develop a relationship with them and potentially enroll them in your group. If you're offering a webinar or teleseminar, consider teaching 1 key section from your full structured group program. Or, ask yourself what information, tools or inspiration is your ideal group participant looking for? You want to make sure you're offering something through your sign-up page that will pre-qualify registrants, meaning if they sign up for this, you *know* they are someone who may be interested in your group.

See the Creating Your Content section for tips on what to present in your webinar.

Designing Your Opt-In Page: When creating an opt-in page, keep it extremely clean with no more than two colors (plus background color) and no more than two fonts. Make sure you include the following **5 keys to a successful opt-in page**, and do NOT include much else, as it causes distraction. Including an introductory video is often a great addition.

1. A compelling headline (Catch their attention.)
2. 3–5 benefits (Focus on what they will learn or take away from your free giveaway.)
3. A call-to-action (Make the offer.)
4. An email opt-in form (Collect their name and email in exchange for the offer.)
5. Social proof (Share client testimonials, tweets, or posts.)

We've included <u>*Opt-In Page*</u> *best practices and tips to give you an idea of successful layouts!*

Marketing Your Opt-In Page: There are a variety of methods to get *New* prospects to visit your Opt-In Page. You can do paid advertising on Facebook, Google, etc. You can attend networking groups, participate in a telesummit (where you are a speaker), or collaborate with a joint venture partner who will promote your entry-level program to their list.

Calls-To-Action:

Calls-to-actions use directive words, such as *register, call, today, now,* etc. Most people have a difficult time making decisions, even if they are highly interested in the outcomes of the decision. There will be people who really want to join your group but have a number of reasons they are trying to talk themselves out of it. Without a call-to-action, many people—even if they're excited about it—will choose to give into their resistance rather than moving forward. And once they leave, their enthusiasm will wane as they get distracted with life. Why do you think car salesmen are so pushy? Because very few people who walk off the lot ever return. It's the same for your webinar.

(We recognize most coaches do not like feeling "salesy"... neither do we! But, a well-structured call-to-action offers value to the audience that they lose out on if they don't make it. If you do not offer participants an opportunity to work with you, you are doing them a DIS-service!)

Below are 3 types of calls-to-action:

- **Time based**—"Last chance to get ____ at the $xx early bird registration!"

- **Limiter**—"The first x number who join receive a special bonus…" or "Only X spaces left!"

- **Decisive action**—"Join today by___ and get XYZ___ act now!" or "We reward decisiveness and if you join in the next _____ you receive ____." (Other common phrases are "fast action scholarship" or "today only.")

Email Campaigns Using Autoresponders:

An autoresponder allows you to pre-schedule a follow-up sequence of emails. This is important because, as mentioned, many people will not sign up right away, such as during your webinar. Plus, a large number of the people who opt-in to webinars do not show up. The largest percentage of people need multiple contacts before they act. Using an autoresponder is a great way to do this. There are many different uses for these advanced email systems and different ways to use autoresponders. But we provide you a sample autoresponder sequence outline here that you can use when you first announce a group, whether you're inviting your own list or you're inviting webinar attendees.

An autoresponder allows you to pre-schedule email responses and sequences. This allows you to design a **marketing campaign** that slowly courts your leads. There are two types of autoresponder services:

- **Basic Autoresponders** (automatic emails that go up when a user registers, and continue a pre-designed sequence by date)

- **Responsive Campaigns** (a sequence that is triggered to go out based on the individual customer's behavior, interests, and previous sales)

Sample basic email follow-up autoresponder sequence:

Ideally, you'll use an email program that automatically determines which leads have *not* registered and allows you to create pre-programmed emails that will go out to everyone on the list on the dates listed below. However, it is possible to manually maintain your list and send these emails by hand each day.

- Day 14 (14 days before the group begins): Announce group. Tell what it's about, the benefits, and what you want them to do (call-to-action). Much of this could be taken from your Sales Page.

- Day 11: Value + reminder. Provide an article or other information that would be highly interesting to your prospects and that shows you know what you're talking about. At the end, remind them about the upcoming group.

- Day 7: Success Story or Case study. Share an inspirational success story showing how your group program transformed someone's life. Announce an Early Bird registration deadline…

- Day 5: FAQ email. Address the logistical aspects of the group (where, time, weeks, etc.) as well as address concerns that those who are interested may have (how it works, how it applies to them, what happens if they can't make sessions, etc.—examples below)

  - All sessions are recorded and available for replay

  - Weekly emails with video and action assignments between calls

  - Email questions to have them answered on group calls

  - Private Facebook group

- Day 3: Checking-In or *Call Me*. Let them know you've noticed they haven't registered and you want to make sure they saw it and don't miss out. Then, make yourself available to answer questions, whether through a quick conference call or literally put in your phone number and let them call you. Let them know you want to help them determine if it's right for them.

- Day 1: Last Chance (the day the group begins). Remind them they need to get in now or program will start. This is another reason it's important to have groups run on a cycle and not be open enrollment.

For additional training and tools to develop your marketing material, including website copy, checkout our course Write Epic Marketing and Sales Copy. *Find out more at the end of the book.*

6 TIPS FOR CREATING EFFECTIVE SALES PAGES

1) How much copy?

The amount of copy you need depends on the complexity and cost of the product. The more complicated and/or expensive the product, the more you need to explain, show, educate, convince. Include everything that your site visitors might be interested to know or concerned about. You want to overcome all resistance before they get to the bottom of your page. At the end, we've included a basic template of content that you should include in your sales page.

2) Buyers are readers

Worried that your copy is too long? Don't. If somebody is ready to buy after just a brief skim, they can just skip ahead and click *"buy."* On the other hand, if someone reads everything on your site and still has questions and doubts, you lose them. That's why long-form copy works.

Most people won't read it all. But, the ones who do are the most likely to buy.

3) Avoid cheesy and scammy copy

Exclamation marks! False HYPE! Don't do it. See below.

Learn to Make Money Using Your Digital Camera & Computer
for less than $40!

Hands down this is THE Absolute Best Small Business Offer On-Line!

Are you ready to own a business buy don't know where to start?

Get paid to help protect people from the devastation of robbery, earthquake, tornado, hurricane, fire, death, divorce, and life's mishaps.

If you are honest and ready to make your mark, look no further!
Become an Expert by learning from The Expert!

Writing a whole paragraph as a headline... don't do it!

> **"As An Adult, The Most Crucial Life Skill You'll EVER Discover Is How To Influence ANY Hiring Manager To Offer You A High-paying Job With A Success-sized Salary... To Take Your Purchasing Power And Lifestyle To An Amazing New Level (That Will Make Others Envy You As They Struggle To Make Ends Meet)... And Here's EXACTLY How To Do IT..."**
>
> *In About 5 Minutes Of Reading This VERY Important Letter, You'll Be Learning The Exact 5-Step Secret Formula For Getting A High-Income Job In ANY ECONOMY That Has Taken Me YEARS To Discover...*
>
> **Dear Experienced Worker Looking For A High-paying Job,**
>
> I have some questions for you:
>
> • Have you been avoiding the question of looking for a better-paying job, simply

4) It's all about the content

Long form sales pages are mostly about the content. You can only write excellent copy if you understand your target audience.

Copywriting Keys to Success:

- Write as if you are speaking directly to your tribe of ideal participants. Use their language and the word **you**.

- Use a friendly, conversational tone. Write as if you were talking to a good friend.

- Speak directly about their challenges from a place of empathy and understanding. Make them feel you *get them* and you've been in their shoes.

Your copy also needs to be structured and designed well. Below are tips for text structure:

- Large font size (minimum 16px).
- Short lines (40 to 80 characters per line).
- New paragraph every 3–4 lines.
- Use lists, quotes, tables—mix it up.
- Sub-headlines every 2–3 paragraphs.

This wall of text is not going to entice anyone to read:

You THOUGHT you Knew!

Has ONE man EVER told you the Truth?

NO!! Not ONE man has ever told you the truth about how men really think about women!! NO ONE!!

You may have heard about it, but now you have actually found the **Top Secret** Universal Truth About Men. It is so underground, so black ops that the author can't reveal his true identity. **NO** women knows the all the Secrets of the Universal Truth About Men! We just call it, "The UTAM". And very few women know ANY of the truths that men are just completely unwilling to divulge. **Absolutely NO** Woman knows! But every woman NEEDS to know what drives men. They NEED to know the closest held secrets that a man will NEVER tell a woman. If you find out the inner workings of the male brain when it comes to how we think about women, it will forever change how you perceive men. It will give you a peek under the hood of the male psyche. And I guarantee you, this is the very FIRST TIME this information has been made available to women. All men know this stuff, but would NEVER reveal it to a woman.

That's OK. You Can Stay Ignorant.

You don't **HAVE** to know these secrets. You don't have to **ever** find out what really makes a man tick. But those women who do read the UTAM **will** know. And I'm not sure **they** will tell you either once they learn. They may want to keep it for themselves in order to have a leg up on other women. **Why won't men tell you about the UTAM?** In the first place, it is somewhat embarrassing that we are so conniving and devious. It's not the kind of information you go around telling people about yourself. You have NO IDEA about some of the tactics men use to seduce women, as well as other ploys.

And secondly, if we told you all the secrets of the UTAM, obviously it would be more difficult to employ its tactics.

Are you searching for a way of **Understanding Men**? Are you looking for some of the secrets about men that will help you with dating men? Although the UTAM does contain **dating advice**, and **relationship advice for women**, it focuses mainly on what men are thinking about when they are around women. Do you really want to know **What Men Want**?

Within the **Universal Truth About Men** are the secrets that almost all men know, but NEVER reveal or discuss except when talking with their absolute best buddies. And some men won't even admit these concepts to anyone but themselves, being a bit ashamed to admit to anyone how they really feel. **ALL** women want to know this information about men. But **NO** man wants women to discover these deepest, darkest secrets about themselves and their fellow males. However, no less than 90% of all men use these Universal Truths tactics, but would **NEVER** explain them to a woman.

The majority of users will only read the headlines and sub-headlines, which gives them the gist of the information.

5) Consider adding video

While video can boost conversions, in most cases, video should not replace text. Most people will *Not* watch the video (but the most interested people might), so the text content should be created with this in mind.

6) Don't encourage them to leave the page

Sometimes, you have additional information you wish to provide, but do not include a link to an outside page… keep them on the page. There are different ways to include additional information. **For example you can expand/collapse information.** With FAQs, when a visitor clicks on a question, have it expand to show the answer. This design helps you make the page shorter while providing additional information.

Answers to frequently asked questions

– What specifically will I learn from this product?

You will learn how to get more leads, traffic and sales using the world's largest professional networking site... LinkedIn. You will also learn how to get the job of your dreams, promote live and virtual events and "fill your stadium", network with high level investors and decision makers, build large targeted communities with groups, and much more.

+ How will this product teach me to generate business leads?

+ How can this product benefit an independent professional like me?

+ How can this product benefit a small business or corporation?

Check out this site for an example of an epic sales page: www.renegadedietbook.com/

Your sales page doesn't need to be held to *that* high of a standard—this is one of the best of the best—but looking at it for inspiration is a great way to get inspiration and aim for excellence!

Sales Page Content Template

Use the template on the following page to create the copy for your sales page. Even if you do not create a sales page, this information can be used in marketing material or discussed during a strategy session.

Additional Elements to Include:

- Your Picture
- Testimonials
- Audio or video greeting

For additional training and tools to develop your marketing material, including website copy, checkout our course Write Epic Marketing and Sales Copy. *Find out more at the end of the book.*

Results-Oriented Headline

Their Challenges and Obstacles

What's Possible: Their Desired Outcomes and Results

Your Story (Vulnerability, Struggles, Search, Solution and Your Expertise/Credibility)

Description of Coaching Group (What They'll Get, Do and Learn, the Outcomes They Will Receive... "So that you can...")

Who the Group is for ("This is for you if...")

Benefits of Group Coaching

Details and Logistics of the Coaching Group

Price Justification (How much other programs cost in comparison, how much your one-on-one coaching costs in comparison, how much time, energy and money you've invested to gain the mastery in this area that they'll be getting access to, how much money, time or headache it will save them.)

Bonuses

Guarantee (Offering a 100% money back guarantee takes the risk away and increases sign-ups. Important to determine how long it is available, such as by the end of the first session, 2nd session, first month, etc)

Address Their Objections and Concerns (Frequently Asked Questions)

Urgency (Include a Limiter)

Recap (Summarize Key Benefits, What They Receive)

Call-to-Action (Tell Them Exactly What to Do)

7 TIPS FOR EFFECTIVE OPT-IN/ LANDING PAGES

1) Remove the Main Navigation

Once a visitor arrives on a landing page, it's your job to keep them there. So if there are links on the page that enable visitors to move about your website, you run the risk of distracting them.

2) Match the Headline of the Page to its Corresponding CTA

Keep your messaging consistent in both your call-to-action (CTA) and the headline of the landing page. If people click on a CTA for a free offer only to find out there's a catch on the landing page, you'll instantly lose their trust.

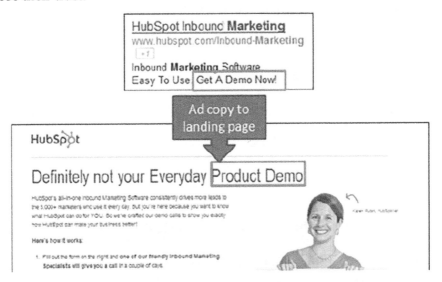

3) Remember: Less Is More

A cluttered page usually results in a distracted, confused, and/or overwhelmed visitor.

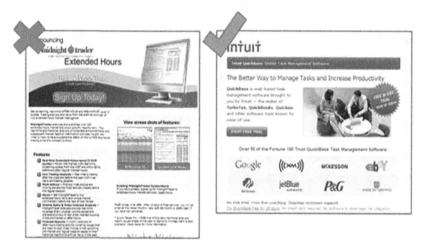

4) Emphasize the Offer's Value

Highlight the benefits of the offer with a brief paragraph or a few bullet points. The best landing page also gives visitors a compelling incentive to download. For example, instead of "Includes specifications of product XYZ," say something along the lines of, "Find out how XYZ can increase productivity by 50%." In other words, emphasize how the offer addresses a specific problem, need, or interest your target audience cares about.

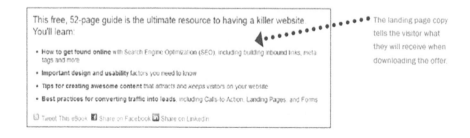

5) Only Ask for the Information You Really Need

In general, the fewer fields you have on a form, the higher the conversion rate. This is because, with each new field you add to a form, it creates more work for the visitor, and thus fewer conversions. (Name, Email and other required information only.)

6) Change *Submit* into a Call-to-Action

If you think about it, no one wants to "submit" to anything. Instead, turn the statement into a call-to-action, such as "Get Your Free Ebook." Here's another helpful tip: Make the button big, bold, and colorful, and make sure it looks like a button, which is usually beveled and appears "clickable."

7) Show Them They're Protected and You're Legit

People are even more resistant to give up their personal information now than ever before. It's understandable, considering all the spam out there. Add a privacy message (or a link to your privacy policy), include security seals, and include social proof, such as testimonials or customer logos.

Example of security seals at the bottom of a landing page form.

SAMPLE OPT-IN/LANDING PAGE

During this FREE webinar, you will learn:

Mia Moran envisions a world where kids crave salads, moms feel healthy and energetic all day, and the whole family feels fabulous after every meal. A gluten-free, vegan lifestyle expert and award-winning graphic designer, Mia guides busy parents to make simple changes for lifelong health and happiness, and help their families do the same.

Congratulations! You made it through the steps to design and structure your life coaching group, develop the professional group facilitator skills, and create a plan for getting your program out into the world where you can make a difference in the lives you are meant to make!

There are a lot of steps to creating, launching and filling groups, so if you haven't already gone through and done all of the activities in this book, keep moving forward! If you want some help finishing this process, check out the online course version of this book!

We are cheering you on! Thank you for transforming with us.

TAKE THE
ONLINE
COURSE!

Learn directly from coach trainers Joeel & Natalie!

The Group Life Coach Certification course covers the content in this book through video lectures and printable worksheets that bring the content in this book to life! Not only is this a GREAT, fun way to review and learn the material, but you will also receive and official **Group Life Coach CERTIFICATION** when you complete the course!

ENROLL FOR ONLY $97!

(That's <50% off!)

Enroll today at **www.transformationacademy.com/groupcoach**

Use coupon code: **groupbook97**

PLUS, **save 50%** on the other courses mentioned in this book!

Use coupon code: **groupbook50**

- Target Marketing: Identify Your Tribe and Niche
- Write Epic Marketing and Sales Copy
- Get Life Coaching Clients with Workshops

MEET THE AUTHORS:

Joeel & Natalie Rivera

Joeel and Natalie Rivera are freedom junkies and prolific content creators who have launched over a dozen business. They have also been coaching, speaking, writing, and teaching for more than a decade.

Through their online education company Transformation Academy, they empower life coaches, INDIEpreneurs and transformation junkies to create a purpose-driven life and business and master the power of their mind so they can create their destiny.

Joeel is a former psychology professor with a Master's Degree in Counseling and Education and has been studying happiness for his dissertation for a Ph.D. in Psychology.

After almost losing it all in 2014 due to a sudden illness after traveling overseas, they converted their workshops, coaching and training programs into online courses. Today, they've created more than 85 online courses, taken by more than 750,000 students from 200 countries (at the time of this writing).

They believe that entrepreneurship is the ultimate form of empowerment. They believe in turning pain into purpose. And, they believe in the democratization of education and, therefore, make their programs available at a price that is within reach of students worldwide.

WWW.TRANSFORMATIONACADEMY.COM

Notes